Above, 111th FIS F-86D 52-3802 from Ellington AFB, Houston, TX, in flight in February 1958. The aircraft's belly is painted aircraft gray for corrosion control. (Texas ANG 111th FIS/147th FW via Mitchell Hail)

F-86D/L DELIVERIES TO THE AIR NATIONAL GUARD

As Convair F-102A, and later F-106A, interceptors became available to the Air Defense Command, USAF F-86Ds began to filter down to the Air National Guard (ANG) units, but it was not until 1957 that sufficient surplus aircraft were available to begin the process. First unit to receive F-86Ds was the 173rd FIS Nebraska ANG, based at Lincoln Municipal Airport. The squadron received F-86Ds in May 1957, converting from F-80C Shooting Stars. Also during 1957, the 111th and the 181st FIS Texas ANG squadrons received F-86Ds, along with the 125th and the 185th FIS Oklahoma ANG. Ten ANG squadrons had received F-86Ds by May 1958, but by this time F-86Ls had also become available, and a number of other Guard squadrons converted straight onto this aircraft without receiving any D-models.

The first ANG F-86L unit was the 108th FIS Illinois ANG, based at O'Hare International Airport. The squadron gained its first aircraft in December 1957, having previously flown the F-84F. National Guard F-86Ds were gradually phased out in 1960, the 196th FIS California ANG flying on with the "Dog" until March 1961, having received F-86Ls in the previous month. Flying only F-86Ds, the 198th FIS Puerto Rico ANG re-equipped with the type in February 1959 and flew these until November 1960. Conversely, the 199th FIS Hawaii ANG operated only F-86Ls, and gained aircraft specially converted for the squadron from December 1957. Like their Air Force counterparts, the ANG F-86Ls were ultimately replaced by the F-102A Delta Dagger, and in the 1960/61 period, many squadrons finally lost their Sabres for good. By early 1962, only six F-86L units remained in ANG service: the 124th FIS Iowa ANG, the 173rd FIS Nebraska ANG, the 181st FIS Texas ANG, the 190th FIS Idaho ANG, the 194th FIS California ANG and the 196th FIS California ANG. The 196th became the last unit to operate the type, converting to F-102s in the summer of 1965.

197TH FIGHTER INTERCEPTOR SQUADRON ARIZONA ANG

The 197th FIS began converting from F-86As in March 1958 at Skyharbor Airport, Phoenix. The unit received F-86Ls mainly from the 329th FIS at George AFB when the latter converted to the F-102A. The F-86Ls in turn began to be replaced by F-104A Starfighters in April 1960. The last Sabres left Phoenix in July of that year, inevitably bound for Davis-Monthan.

At top, first colors worn by 197th FIS F-86Ls were similar to the earlier F-86A scheme. "Copperhead" snake on the fuselage side was yellow outlined by red. 53-4034 was seen at the Luke AFB Armed Forces Day display in May 1958 shortly after receiving its first F-86L. (Brian Baker) Above, 53-828 bellied into Phoenix in 1960 and was subsequently scrapped. The "Copperhead" design was removed from the fuselage side when the high-viz scheme was applied. Instead, a stylized snake's head was placed on the tail fin, above which was painted "Copperheads" in yellow. (Brian Baker)

196th FIS

194TH FIGHTER INTERCEPTOR SQUADRON CALIFORNIA ANG

Based at Fresno, CA, the 194th FIS flew F-86A Sabres until these began to be replaced with F-86Ls in December 1957. Further deliveries came from the 78th FIW at Hamilton AFB in early 1958, the last F-86As leaving in February 1958.

Toward the end of 1964, remaining F-86Ls were ferried in groups of four out to Davis-Monthan for storage; they were replaced by F-102A Delta Daggers.

However, when the last four aircraft came to be flown out of Fresno in December 1964, aircraft 53-642

ost oil pressure on its number 1 ngine bearing and never made it. One week later 53-642 was placed on isplay at Fresno, where it remains to his day.

At top, 52-4278 at NAS Moffett on 21 May 1960. An F-86L-50 from the 194th FIS at Fresno was unusual in having nose art. "Easy Valley Girl" was assigned to Capt. R. G. Hollring. (William Swisher) Above, 194th F-86L-60 53-4050 on 3 October 1962 had da-glo orange nose and rear fuselage stripes. 194th aircraft originally had a yellow chevron outlined in blue on the tail. Fin tip is red. (W. Swisher) Bottom, 194th F-86L-45 52-4197 at NAS Oakland on 3 October 1962. (William Swisher)

196TH FIGHTER INTERCEPTOR SQUADRON CALIFORNIA ANG

Based at Ontario, CA, the 196th FIS had flown the F-86A since March 1954. Conversion to the F-86D began in late September 1958 (although a small number of F-86Ds, including 52-3712, 52-3785 and 52-3876, had been assigned the previous May) and these aircraft were a mixture of F-86D-36 and –41 Sabres. Delivery was completed in October, and the last F-86As left the squadron late in 1958. This initial delivery of F-86Ds to the 196th FIS came entirely from overhaul at McClellan AFB.

In June 1959, a large number of F-86D-41s were passed to the 196th FIS from the 111th FIS at Ellington, TX, and this allowed the former to get rid of all the F-86D-36s and some of the D-41s concurrently. Thus, the squadron was able to briefly standardize on the F-86D-41 and the logistics support of these aircraft was considerably simplified.

Re-equipment with the F-86L was a far smoother affair – all aircraft were assigned to 196th FIS in February 1961 from the 128th FIS at Dobbins AFB. In the first week of March 1961, the last F-86Ds were ferried out to Davis-Monthan for storage. The F-86Ls were finally replaced by F-102As in early 1965. The 196th FIS was the last ANG F-86D/L squadron.

At top, 194th F-86L-55 53-0642 at Fresno on 21 January 1965 after retirement which became one of the Fresno's display aircraft. The fin tip and wing tip were dark blue and all the da-glo finish had been removed. (Swisher) Above, unmarked 196th F-86L-60 53-0897 at Ontario Airport on 25 June 1962. (D. Kasulka via Norm Taylor) Below, two Ontario-based 196th FIS Sabre Dogs in flight wearing da-glo markings. (via Don Spering, Aircraft in Review)

4

above, 196th FIS California ANG F-86L-60 53-897 in fresh (unfaded) da-glo markings at Ontario in 1962. The fin tip was yellow and the anti-glare panel black. The radome was faded to tan. (Ron Picciani via Isham) At right, late 96th FIS markings consisted of the ANG logo on the tail with CALIFORNIA written above it. Silver lacquer finish and aluminized lacquer undersides were typical of the Sabre Dog's final years. 52-10170 was donated to the town of Montclair. (William Swisher)

Above, F-86Ds flown by the 120th FIS wore nondescript markings only relieved by COLO ANG script. 52-3604 was flown by the unit from May 1958 through February 1960 when it was replaced by an F-86L. (W. Swisher)

20TH FIGHTER SQUADRON COLORADO ANG

The 120th FIS was based at Denver (later Buckley ANG Base), and flew F-86Es (operated by the accomplished Minute Men aerobatic team) until the summer of 1958. During May of 1958, the first F-86Ds arrived from McClellan AFB to restore the squadron to full strength; the aerobatic team was dropped at this time.

In January 1960, the 120th FIS began to convert to the F-86L, and the old D models were retired to Davis-Monthan by the end of March. The majority of the new F-86Ls came from the 133rd FIS NH ANG, and were retained for just one year before being replaced with F-100Cs in January 1961. At that time the unit became a Tactical Fighter Squadron

and the last Sabres left for Davis-Monthan in April of that year.

Above, when Colorado received the F-86L, it adopted the colorful da-glo scheme augmented by fuselage and tail flashes outlined in yellow. F-86L-5 53-726 had red flashes and drop tank noses for red flight. (Fred Roos) At left, F-86L 53-889, seen at Peterson AFB, had blue flashes and drop tank noses for blue flight. (H. W. Rued via Mart Isham)

Above, 159th's simple but smart blue and white tail markings were carried over to the unit's F-106s. Seen here on 25 January 1958, 51-5942 served with the unit since August 1956. (Swisher)

159TH FIGHTER INTERCEPTOR SQUADRON FLORIDA ANG

Florida's 159th FIS based at Imeson Field flew F-80C Shooting Stars from 1955. On 1 July of 1956, the unit's first F-86D, 51-5915, arrived from Fresno. By the end of August nine F-86Ds had arrived from NAA's Fresno line, though all subsequent deliveries came from McClellan AFB. The 159th FIS operated twenty-five Sabre Dogs – all F-86D-26 models.

These F-86Ds were retained until mid-June of 1959 when they began to be ferried out for storage at Davis-Monthan. Concurrently, on 19 June 1959, the first F-86Ls were assigned to the 159th FIS, from the 329th Consolidated Logistics Maintenance

Squadron at Stewart AFB. The unit was fully re-equipped by the end of July. The last three F-86Ds departed for storage on 16 July, although 51

6

5908 was retained until 22 July and donated to the town of Gulfport, Missouri, for display.

The replacement F-86Ls did not serve for long, however, and Convair F-102As arrived in June 1960. The final Sabres had left by the end of March.

128TH FIGHTER INTERCEPTOR SQUADRON GEORGIA ANG

The 128th FIS squadron, at Dobbins AFB, began converting from the F-84F to the F-86L during July 1958. On 1 April 1961, the unit became a transport squadron equipped with C-97Fs. The last Sabres had been flown to the 196th FIS at Ontario Airport, CA, in February 1961.

Above, Florida ANG F-86D-26s 51-5861, 51-5901 and 51-5896 in flight over Florida in late 1959. (FL ANG via Norm Taylor)

Below, four 128th FIS Georgia ANG F-86Ls (53-606, 51-098, 53-651, & 53-742) from Dobbins AFB in flight. The aircraft wore a yellow/orange triangle on the tail outlined in black, along with the squadron insignia. (Georgia ANG via Norm Taylor)

158TH FIGHTER INTERCEPTOR SQUADRON GEORGIA ANG

Based at Travis Field, Savannah, GA, the 158th FIS flew F-84F Thunderstreaks until late 1958 when F-86Ls began to arrive with the unit. The first such aircraft were assigned from McClellan AFB on 10 December 1958. The last Sabre arrived in June 1959. The squadron's parent organization, the 165th Fighter Group, had been federally recognized on 10 July 1958.

On 1 April 1962, the unit took over a cargo-hauling role, and on the same date became the 158th Air Transport Squadron. It then began to receive C-97F Stratofreighters, but

Above, 128th FIS F-86L-55 53-563 a Dobbins AFB, GA, in June 1960. The 128th did not share the da-glo mark ings of its sister squadron, the 158th FIS seen below. (116th TFW, GA ANG via Norm Taylor) Below, the 158th FIS wore a red triangle on the tail and ha da-glo nose, rear fuselage and oute wing panel markings. Note rebel fla on the nose. (via Lionel Paul)

the last Sabres did not leave unt July. Most went to Davis-Monthan fo storage, but a few were ferried t Wright-Patterson AFB on 5 Ma 1962, where they were declare excess and donated to local towns.

199TH FIGHTER INTERCEPTOR SQUADRON HAWAII ANG

The 199th FIS was unique in receiving F-86Ls straight from the conversion line – all other ANG units received the type second-hand from service with USAF units. All of the aircraft were converted at North American's Inglewood plant, and were shipped across the Pacific from San Francisco. They arrived in Hawaii on 28 January 1958 and were immediately assigned to the 6486th Air Base Wing at Hickam AFB for depreservation prior to use by the 199th FIS.

Previously, the Hawaii ANG had flown F-86Es, and these aircraft were retained until the F-86Ls were slowly filtered into the squadron. The first F-86L was assigned from the 6486th ABW on 5 February 1958. But it was not until July that the final aircraft entered service with the 199th FIS. The F-86Es were retired in June and scrapped on site.

The F-86Ls were then replaced in January 1961 by F-102As, though

Above, HANG F-86L 52-4191 after retirement at Honolulu International in 1968. Tail checkerboard was red and yellow-orange as was the fuselage stripe. (Nick Williams) Below, F-86L 52-4174 in flight with its replacement, the F-102A in May 1961. (via D. Curtis)

conversion was again quite slow, and the last Sabres were not lost until May of that year. As with the F-86Es, they were scrapped on site.

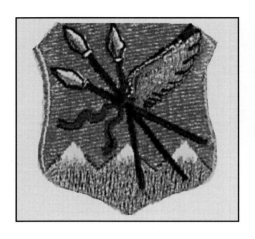

Above, Idaho ANG F-86Ls originally had da-glo nose, rear fuselage and outer wing panel trim outlined in black. The aircraft also has a yellow tail band. (Picciani via Isham) Below, F-86L 53-3696 on 22 March 1965 in Idaho's final Dog scheme sans da-glo, wears an ANG badge on the tail with IDAHO written above it. Crew chief was S/Sgt B. Fisher and pilot was Maj D. J. Abbott. (William Swisher)

190TH FIGHTER INTERCEPTOR SQUADRON IDAHO ANG

Flying from Gowen Field, Boise, ID, the 190th FIS converted from F-89B Scorpions starting in April 1959, although aircraft were only slowly assigned. By the end of October the unit was finally at full strength. The squadron converted to F-102As early in 1964, and lost its last F-86L to Davis-Monthan in April.

Early 108th FIS F-86Ls had bland markings devoid of color or of unit or individual markings. Above, F-86L-55 53-0564 on 2 June 1958 with the last three digits of the serial number 564 on the nose gear door. (Dave Menard via Norm Taylor) Below, F-86L-55 53-697 at Peoria, IL, on 15 May 1959. (Dave Menard via Norm Taylor)

108TH FIGHTER INTERCEPTOR SQUADRON ILLINOIS ANG

The 108th FIS converted from F-84Fs in November 1957 at O'Hare International Airport, receiving its first F-86Ls in November. The 108th was notable in being the first National Guard unit to equip with the F-86L, all of which were gained from the 56th FG at O'Hare. On 1 April 1961, the unit transferred to the air refuelling role, and gained KC-97F tankers. The last Sabres departed, mainly to storage at Davis-Monthan during, July of the same year.

Starting in late 1959, 108th F-86Ls acquired da-glo trim and a blue tail band over which the unit's badge was applied. Above, all aircraft had a color coded flight band beneath the blue tail band; in the case of 52-10155 it was red as was the drop tank trim. A squirrel has been painted on the nose gear door. (via Lionel Paul) At right, F-86L-50 52-10101 at O'Hare on 1 February 1960 with a red flight stripe on the tail. Drop tanks had red trim outlined in white. The nose gear door was da-glo with a red number one outlined in black. (Paul Stevens via N. Taylor) At right, F-86L-55 53-637 on 8 January 1961 had a yellow flight stripe outlined in black on the tail with the colors repeated on the aircraft's drop tanks. Nose gear door and drop tank fins had red and white stripes. (Paul Stevens via Don Spering) Bottom, 53-704 on 21 November 1960 had a blue flight stripe on the tail, a red nose gear door and red and white drop tank stripes. The da-glo trim was outlined in black. (Paul Stevens via Norm Taylor)

124TH FIGHTER INTERCEPTOR SQUADRON IOWA ANG

Flying from Des Moines, the 124th FIS started converting from F-84E Thunderjets with the arrival of its first F-86L in June 1958. The Sabres were operated for four years, and were replaced by F-89J Scorpions starting in April 1962, with most F-86Ls being transferred out to Davis-Monthan in the same month. Many ex-124th FIS Sabres subsequently went to the Royal Thai AF.

Iowa ANG F-86Ls wore a red-bordered pale green tail band with unit badge and da-glo trim. At top, F-86L-60 53-843 has a red intake stripe on 23 June 1960. (P. Stevens via Taylor) Above right, F-86L-55 53-750 on 23 June 1960. (P. Stevens via D. Spering) At right, F-86L-60 53-862. (via Lionel Paul) Below, F-86L-60 53-877 at Des Moines on 23 June 1960. (P. Stevens via Fred Roos)

122ND FIGHTER INTERCEPTOR SQUADRON LOUISIANA ANG

Previously operating F-80Cs from Gulfport, Mississippi, the 122nd FIS received its first F-86D in October 1957 (from Nebraska's 173rd FIS) in order that squadron personnel could become accustomed to the aircraft. However, this first Sabre was actually received at the unit's home base in New Orleans as engine mechanic "Goody" Goodrich explains:

"The [first] F-86 flew in for a 'show and tell' so the troops could get an idea of what it looked like, points of service and things like that. We shared a hangar on a civilian airport, which was called New Orleans Airport, which protrudes out into Lake Pontchartrain. We shared the hangar with the Army National Guard. We were flying F-80s and T-birds out of Gulfport, which was an old WWII military field in Mississippi because the runway at New Orleans Airport was only 4500 to 5000 feet in length. Thank goodness when they decided to fly the '86 in, the drag chute worked and they were able to get it stopped in time."

"They brought it in the hangar, and we'd hired quite a few boys with ex-Air Force service that had worked the D's so they were giving us a demonstration of the different points of service. There was one particular utility reservoir up on the backbone behind the canopy that was pressurised and he even

made mention, 'Make sure you relieve the pressure before you remove the cap'. Well, in his zeal to show his intelligence and his knowledge of the aircraft, he did exactly the opposite of what he'd said to do. He popped the cap and we had about 2 gallons of fluid running all over the place."

"After the 'show and tell', which was on a weekend drill, the aircraft was going to go back to Gulfport because we were starting to receive them over there one at a time. The only problem was that to get it out, we could only put about a third of the fuel load aboard to make sure that the aircraft was light enough that it could get off that 4800-ft runway - which it did. All our other training and schooling in receipt of aircraft was accomplished at Alvin Callender Field, which is south of New Orleans at Belle Chasse, Louisiana. This was built as a joint reserve-training base. We had Navy, Navy Reserve, AFRES, Air Guard, Marine Reserve, Coast Guard – you name it, we had some of it there."

As Goody indicates, the unit moved out to Alvin Callender

Above, the 122nd accepted its first F-86Ls in January 1960. However, the acceptance ceremony didn't take place until the following month. Pictured above, during that ceremony at Callender Field, is 52-4264 in the foreground still wearing 157th FIS markings. At right, behind the speaker, is F-86L 52-3749 in 122nd markings. The tail arrowhead was blue with three white stars and a yellow half moon. (Don Goodrich)

Field/NAS New Orleans and this was accomplished on 5 December 1957. The majority of F-86Ds actually arrived in February 1958, allowing the last F-80s to depart for storage. However, despite receiving more modern aircraft, the maintenance crews in particular had their work cut out. As an example, no engine test facility existed at Callender Field, so all engine testing and leak checking was done installed in the aircraft. And if a problem occurred, the engine usually had to be removed again for rectification; accessibility was not a trait of the "Dog". On the F-86D, the radar/fire control and engine men were probably hardest-worked:

"It wasn't until we got down to Callender that we actually started

our schooling on the '86. Everybody went through school and then you split off into whatever your speciality was going to be - either airframe or engine, hydraulics, whatever. Mine wound up to be engine, which I stayed with until I retired in '91. I totally enjoyed my experience. I saw a lot of changes in the evolution from 1956 until 1991 but I can't say I'd go back and change any of it. It was definitely an experience that most people don't get a chance to go through."

"Our maintenance system was broken down into different entities. We worked strictly engine – once it was either in or out of the aircraft, but they had the other shop for the electronic fuel control that was called the IEC – Integrated Engine Control. They did all the testing and troubleshooting for the electronic fuel scheduling system for the J47. We would change the main engine component, but they would do all the settings for temperature, max. RPM and nozzle [position]."

"Talking of nozzles, it did have a strange burner assembly on it. It had a burner that looked just like two clamshells that would close off the exhaust nozzle for 'military' [thrust] and swing to the sides for when they initiated burner. The nozzle arrangement was electrically actuator driven, the actuator

was mounted in the six o'clock position on the afterburner rear duct."

"Due to the short time that we had the aircraft, our scope of maintenance was limited to only hot section – combustion chamber, nozzle, transition duct, turbine, afterburner and accessory repair and replacement. We didn't get into any compressor rework because we didn't have the tooling and the Air Force figured it was cheaper to just swap engines out (which it was) than to give each unit the tooling to do compressor rework."

"We also did have a problem with multiple flangular circumferential cracks in the burner area. Unfortunately, when we got these we were down at NAS down at Belle Chasse. It took a long time for our supply system to get the appropriate equipment we needed and unfortunately we ran into these duct cracks about ten days before we were supposed to deploy someplace. The only people on base that had a Heliarc welder were the Navy. Consequently, we had to pull the burner off every aircraft and truck it down to the Navy and had our welder - who had gotten checked out by then – go through and re-weld all those flanges."

Unusually for an ANG unit, 122nd FIS almost immediately began apply-

ing unit markings to its aircraft. On the F-86D, this comprised a blue arrow along the fuselage side on which was painted two white stars, two golden yellow bands and a golden yellow crescent. The latter denoted New Orleans, "The Crescent City". On the tail, the arrow design was repeated though this time just three small stars and a crescent were applied.

On 26 January 1960, the 122nd FIS began to receive its first F-86L aircraft, and the last F-86D departed for Davis-Monthan the following month. All F-86Ls came directly from 157th FIS SC ANG at Congaree, but only remained with the unit for a short time. Re-equipment with Convair F-102As began in July of that year and the last Sabres departed for Davis Monthan and 128th FIS GA ANG in September 1960.

During the whole action-packed two years the unit flew the Sabre only a handful were lost in flying accidents, as 'Goody' Goodrich relates:

"We had lost a total in the two-year period of, I think, three '86s. One was lost on takeoff. He had got to about 1500 feet and the engine flamed out. He was able to supposedly make three air re-starts, or attempted, which all failed and he punched out. That's a hell of a lot of times to try to get an engine restarted at 1500 feet, but you can't dispute the pilot. It crashed at an old Navy ordnance depot which was about four miles away. Thankfully, no ordnance was in storage at that point in time."

"Another one we had which was quite spectacular, was that [the

pilot] had a locked control system. The only thing he had was very minimal movement of ailerons and elevators. Basically, he was flying the aircraft with the trim system and managed to get it back in the vicinity of Alvin Callender Field at Belle Chasse. Back in the 1950s there wasn't much down there besides us and the alligators. He came across the south end of the field closest to Navy Ops and we were all out on the ramp. I guess he was at 1500-2000 feet and we could witness a complete ejection sequence. The canopy went, you saw the puff of smoke and fire, and we saw him and the seat go out. [We] saw he had a good separation from him and the seat, except that when he landed, he landed in a tree-line right outside of the base on the south end of the field. In his haste he disconnected his upper harness strap disconnects first and went upside-down. He had to sit there for 15 minutes until Navy Rescue could get to him and cut his crotch straps to get him out. We never did find anything in the wreckage or by duplication that could have caused the lockup of the flight controls. Unfortunately, you have to believe what they're telling you – you're not actually there to actually feel it and see it."

"Another one we lost because the oil pump shaft sheared, depleted the engine of oil and locked it up. All the ejections on the '86 were successful though."

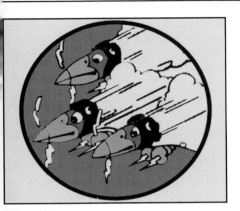

127TH FIGHTER INTERCEPTOR SQUADRON KANSAS ANG

Flying from McConnell AFB, the 127th FIS converted from F-80Cs to F-86Ls in April 1958, though it had received its first Sabre on January 10. Most of these Sabres came from 1st FIW at Selfridge. The unit was redesignated as a TFS on 1 April 1961, converting to F-100C Super Sabres at that time. All surviving Sabres were transferred to Davis-Monthan by the end of the month.

Below, Kansas ANG F-86L-50 52-4256 on display in September 1990 at McConnell AFB wore 127th markings consisting of a yellow tail stripe with a black map of the state painted on it. (Ben Knowles via Isham)

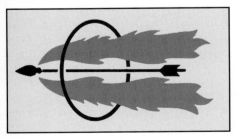

173RD FIGHTER INTERCEPTOR SQUADRON NEBRASKA ANG

Operating F-80Cs from Lincoln Municipal Airport, the 173rd FIS received its first F-86D from the 326th FIS in January 1957. However, it was not until August that the majority of the Sabres arrived. The squadron had been standing ADC runway alert since July 1955, maintaining four aircraft at 24-hour readiness, seven days a week.

However, despite having a brand-new hangar to work out of at Lincoln, the transition from Shooting Star to Sabre was not smooth. Few of the special tools associated with the F-86D ever turned up, and maintenance crews had to manufacture their own. The radar system also caused some problems, mainly caused by an initial lack of trained maintenance personnel on base. These problems had largely been solved by March 1958 when the squadron moved into the

former Navy Reserve hangar area at Lincoln.

Two-week summer camps were taken in during the Sabre period, including trips to Casper, Wyoming, in 1957 and Gulfport, Mississippi, during 1958. Also, in September 1958 Capt Clarence Christensen won the annual Ricks Race, and took the prestigious Ricks Trophy for the 173rd. Christensen and his crew chief had pre- pared his aircraft for weeks before the event, installing a fresh engine and polishing the airframe to achieve opti- mum performance. Thus, when he took off on 21 September for the race itself, he was well-placed for a good finish.

As part of the Ricks Race, Christensen was required to perform a practice intercept near Panama City in Florida, refuel at New Orleans in Louisiana, and sprint to the finish line in Dallas, Texas, 850 miles later. Christensen and his Sabre were just eighteen seconds ahead of the sec- ond place finisher over the line. The whole mission had taken one hour forty-eight minutes and twenty sec- onds.

Starting in September 1959, the F-86Ds were supplanted and replaced by F-86Ls, though the last

At top, belly pod carried under 52-3598 is a radar reflector. Aircraft carries the 173rd's initial markings which includ- ed the squadron insignia on the nose and tail. (Neb. ANG) At left, publicity photo of F-86L 53-949 with squadron CO, Col Fred H. Bailey, at left. Aircraft was lost in a crash at Lincoln on 19 July 1962. (Neb. ANG) Below, 173rd FIS F-86L 51-6140 wears the squadron's second color scheme. Da-glo has been applied to the nose, rear fuselage and outer wing panels and NEBR AIR GUARD was moved to the forward fuselage. The squadron insignia was moved from the nose to the wing tanks and red and white stripes were added to the drop tank fins. (via N. Taylor)

F-86Ds remained until the end of December.

Throughout the Sabre period, the 173rd FIS was commanded by Col Fred H. Bailey, a founding member of the Air National Guard at Lincoln. Incredibly, Bailey led the unit from introduction of P-51 Mustangs until retiring from the Guard in 1980, by which time the 173rd was flying RF-4C Phantom IIs. On 1 July 1960, the 173rd FIS was organized as part of the 155th Fighter Group and personnel increased to over nine hundred. During the Cuban Missile Crisis in 1962 the unit doubled its ADC alert commitment to eight aircraft.

The 173rd FIS remained a Sabre

unit until May 1964, when it became a Tactical Recon unit with RF-84F Thunderflashes. Concurrently, the

ADC alert status was ended and the F-86Ls departed for Davis-Monthan in the same month.

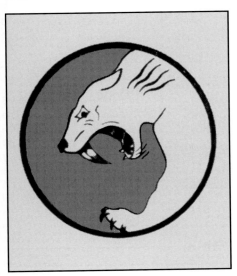

133RD FIGHTER INTERCEPTOR SQUADRON NEW HAMPSHIRE ANG

Based at Grenier Field, the 133rd FIS converted from F-94B Starfires to F-86Ls during February of 1958. However, the last Sabres did not arrive until May to complete conversion onto the type, and this coincided with the withdrawal of the last F-94s to storage. The 133rd FIS then took on the transport role with C-97s starting in September 1960, and the F-86Ls were all reassigned to the 120th FIS. The last Sabres left Grenier in April 1960.

Above, third and final markings applied to 173rd aircraft had U.S. AIR FORCE replacing NEBR AIR GUARD, NEBR relocated to the tail and the Air Guard insignia added to the tail also. The "0" before the serial number 53-904 was added to early '50s aircraft still in service ten years later so as not to confuse them with '60s issued serial numbers. (William Swisher) Below, based at Grenier Field, the 133rd flew the F-86L from February 1958 through September 1960. 52-10150 is seen in 1958 during an open house at Grenier Field in 1958. Aircraft had da-glo markings and a blue tail stripe outlined in green to denote blue flight. Wing tank noses were also blue. (via Craig Kaston)

192ND FIGHTER INTERCEPTOR SQUADRON NEVADA ANG

The 192nd FIS was based at Reno Municipal Airport and was the last ANG F-86A operator. The unit began replacing the F-86As with F-86Ls in August 1958. The first F-86Ls for the 192nd FIS came straight from the 15th FIS at Davis-Monthan. In February 1959, the 192nd FIS started to receive F-86Ls from overhaul at McClellan AFB, and the last F-86As departed in March 1959.

The F-86Ls were replaced in March 1961 when the 192nd became a Tac Recon Squadron with RB-57 Canberras. All Sabres had been ferried to Davis-Monthan by mid-April.

Above, F-86L 52-4150 in da-glo markings with blue fin tip. Tail flash was also blue and was outlined in white. The 133rd also had a blue silhouette of Nevada capped by a banner bearing the legend 152nd FG. Each aircraft's state silhouette contained the name of one of Nevada's cities with a white star indicating its location. In this case the "City of Ely". (via Berger) Below, final 152nd markings were natural metal with ANG emblem on the tail and NEVADA in white on a blue stripe. 53-994 has an Outstanding Unit citation painted on the nose. (via Lionel Paul)

156TH FIGHTER INTERCEPTOR SQUADRON NORTH CAROLINA ANG

Based at Douglas Municipal Airport, the 156th FIS had flown Sabres since January 1954, first the A model, and then from October 1957, the F-86E. The first F-86Ls for the unit arrived during January 1959 and conversion was complete by the end of May. Most of these F-86Ls came direct from overhaul at McClellan AFB.

In January 1961, the unit became an aeromedical airlift squadron with C-119s, and the last Sabres were sent to Davis-Monthan on 30 March of that year.

Above, finished in natural metal overall, F-86L 53-906 was one of the first "Dogs" assigned to the unit. A red state of North Carolina silhouette was painted below the canopy. Another F-86L, 53-832, is at left and it is void of any ANG markings as it was just received by the unit. The squadron's full complement of F-86Es can be seen in the background. (via Barry Miller)

125TH FIGHTER INTERCEPTOR SQUADRON OKLAHOMA ANG

125th FIS converted from F-80Cs to F-86D Sabres in September 1957 at Tulsa, OK. Additionaly, a number of F-86Ls were assigned during January 1960, but all squadron Sabres were flown out that same month with conversion of 125th FIS to Boeing C-97 freighters.

Above, North Carolina ANG F-86L-60 53-919 in September 1960 at Charlotte, NC. 156th FIS aircraft acquired da-glo markings and retained the red state silhouette below the canopy. (Ben Knowles) At right, Oklahoma ANG F-86D-41 51-8491 belonged to the 185th FIS. Tail and drop tank trim was yellow outlined in black. (Brian Baker)

185TH FIGHTER INTERCEPTOR SQUADRON OKLAHOMA ANG

The 185th FIS, based at Will Rogers ANG Base in Oklahoma City, converted from F-80C Shooting Stars to F-86Ds in May 1958. These aircraft came straight from overhaul at McClellan AFB. In the third week of March 1960, all F-86Ds were ferried out to Davis-Monthan, having been replaced with newer F-86Ls.

All F-86Ls for the 185th FIS were assigned straight from the 14th FIS at Sioux City, and arrived starting on 3 March 1960. The unit became a transport squadron with C-97s in April 1961; all remaining Sabres had left for storage at Davis-Monthan during the previous month.

146TH FIGHTER INTERCEPTOR SQUADRON PENNSYLVANIA ANG

Flying out of Greater Pittsburgh Airport, the 146th FIS converted from F-84Fs to F-86Ls starting in December 1957. The majority of these Sabres came directly from the 42nd FIS, which was based across the airfield. In 1960, F-102As began to arrive and during October the F-86Ls began to be ferried out to Davis-Monthan. However, many Sabres were retained by the 146th FIS until April 1961, when these remaining aircraft were transferred to the 147th FIS, PA ANG.

Pennsylvania's 146th FIS and 147th FIS wore identical markings that consisted of standard da-glo colors with PA. AIR GUARD painted on the forward fuselage. Below, F-86L-60 53-831 at Pittsburg Airport. (via Norm Taylor) Bottom, F-86L-60 53-926 stands ready in its alert shed at the Pittsburg Airport during the late '50s. (PA ANG via Fred Roos)

147TH FIGHTER INTERCEPTOR SQUADRON PENNSYLVANIA ANG

The 147th FIS, also based at Greater Pittsburgh Airport, exchanged F-84Fs for F-86Ls beginning in April 1958. However, unlike its sister squadron, the 147th FIS gained Sabres from a variety of USAF units.

In April 1961, the squadron gained a number of F-86Ls from the 146th FIS, but conversion to C-119J transports began concurrently and the last Sabres were ferried out to Davis-Monthan during June 1961.

Above, 146th FIS F-86L-60 53-1023 in 1958 at the Pittsburg Airport. (Peter Bowers via Norm Taylor) Below, three Pennsylvania-based F-86Ls in flight with 52-10164 in the foreground. (PA ANG via Fred Roos) Bottom, 147th FIS F-86L-60 53-807 at the Pittsburg Airport. (via Norm Taylor)

198TH FIGHTER INTERCEPTOR SQUADRON PUERTO RICO ANG

Based at San Juan International Airport, the 198th FIS converted from F-86E Sabres to F-86Ds in February 1959. The new aircraft were gained from McClellan AFB and the 182nd FIS, Texas ANG. Most of the pilots with the 198th FIS were Puerto Rican, with the balance made up of Americans. The maintenance personnel, again mainly of local descent, were trained in the U.S. like other guard units.

One of the first aircraft to arrive, 51-8422, was lost almost immediately. In one of the more bizarre accidents, a land crab crawled into the left main undercarriage bay and prevented the gear from extending on landing.

More extraordinary was the case of 52-3893. The pilot of '893 was returning from the U.S. on 15 August 1959 and, low on fuel over Cuba, tried to make for the US base at Guantanamo. However he ran dry before reaching safety and was forced to land the aircraft in a sugar cane plantation in the province of Chaparra. Understandably, the Cuban authorities were less than happy about the incident, although a team of 4 mechanics from the PR ANG did manage to dismantle the aircraft and put it in a railroad car. However, '893 was never seen again. The pilot returned to Puerto Rico and continued to fly for the PR ANG for some time after this, according to the

198th FIS historian Fernando Daleccio.

In October 1960, the 198th FIS received F-86Hs, and by the end of the following month had ferried out all of the F-86Ds to Davis-Monthan.

At top, 51-8422 was written off following this accident caused when a land crab jammed the main gear. (Fernando Daleccio) Above, 52-3893 force-landed in Cuba on 15 August 1959 after running out of fuel. It was never returned (Fernando Daleccio) Below, da-glo trimmed 52-3738 on 19 March 1963 (William Swisher)

157TH FIGHTER INTERCEPTOR SQUADRON SOUTH CAROLINA ANG

Flying from Congaree Air Base (later re-named McEntire ANG Base), the 157th FIS had operated F-80Cs since January 1955. These were then replaced by F-86Ls from a variety of sources in February 1958, though total conversion was not complete until mid-June.

In February 1960, Lockheed F-104As began to arrive, and had completely replaced the Sabres by the end of the month. The Sabres were all reassigned to the 122nd FIS at New Orleans.

Below, 157th F-86L-50 52-4232 in 1958. (via Norm Taylor) Bottom, F-866L-50 52-4264 with S. C. AIR GUARD replacing SC ANG used previously in front of the Congaree Air Base sign in 1959. (Don Spering, A.I.R. collection)

Above, 157th FIS pilot Lt Hanlin stands next to his mount F-86L-60 53-870 on 15 August 1958 at Travis Field, Savannah, GA. The aircraft is seen in the original squadron markings. Compare these markings to those of the similarly-posed aircraft below. (via Norm Taylor) Below, F-86L-60 53-1064 at McEntire ANGB wears the second style markings applied to 157th aircraft. (Don Spering, A. I. R. collection) Bottom, sixteen F-86Ls, two T-33s, two T-28s and one C-47 are seen on the 157th flight line on 20 November 1959. By this time, da-glo had been added to the aircraft and a tail stripe had been added to the tail which was outlined in black. These tail stripes varied in color to denote the different flights. (via Norm Taylor)

Above, three 157th FIS F-86Ls in flight, two from red flight and one from yellow flight. These aircraft were transferred to the LA ANG in January 1960. 53-625 crashed on 31 March 1960. (SC ANG via Don Spering) At right, alert aircraft on the ramp at Congaree/McEntire AB on 13 October 1959. 53-822 and 53-595 wear red tail stripes and 53-1031 wears a yellow tail stripe. (via Norm Taylor) Below, width of da-glo outer wing panels is evident in this view of F-86L 53-822 being fired up on the 157th ramp on 13 October 1959. (via Norm Taylor)

151ST FIGHTER INTERCEPTOR SQUADRON TENNESSEE ANG

As the second youngest ANG squadron, the 151st FIS only received federal recognition on 15 December 1957, and gained its first F-86Ds from overhaul at McClellan AFB in April 1958. Based at McGhee-Tyson AFB, the 151st then received F-86Ls in October 1959, transferring the Ds out at the same time. The 151st FIS began converting to F-104A Starfighters in early 1960 and flew its Sabres to Davis-Monthan in June.

Below, 151st FIS F-86D-35 51-8417 in da-glo markings at Knoxville, TN, on 9 August 1959. (Jim Hawkins via Norm Taylor) Bottom, highly polished F-86D-41 52-3679 had all da-glo markings removed and the underbelly was painted gray on 2 February 1960. The tail and wing tank stripes were red outlined by white. (Olmstead via McLaren)

26

111TH FIGHTER INTERCEPTOR SQUADRON TEXAS ANG

The 111th FIS converted from F-80C Shooting Stars to the F-86D Sabre beginning in August 1957 at its Ellington Field base. Also, in 1957, T-33 aircraft were acquired and the unit began operation as the Air National Guard Jet Instrument School.

In May 1959, the 147th Fighter Interceptor Group (FIG) was formed and the 111th Fighter Interceptor Squadron became one of six component squadrons. The 111th was assigned to NORAD. New F-86Ls arrived with the unit from June 1959, with the out-going F-86Ds in turn being handed over to the 196th FIS, CA ANG during the same month. The F-86Ls, which came mainly from the 85th FIS at Scott AFB, were replaced by Convair F-102A Delta Daggers in mid-1960. The last Sabres departed Ellington for storage at Davis-Monthan on 20 October 1960.

181ST FIGHTER INTERCEPTOR SQUADRON TEXAS ANG

Based at Hensley ANG Base in Dallas, the 181st FIS converted from F-80C Shooting Stars to F-86D Sabres during September 1957. The Sabre Dogs were gained from overhaul at McClellan AFB and remained until March 1960 when the last aircraft was flown out to Davis-Monthan.

New equipment for the 181st FIS was the F-86L, which had begun to arrive in small numbers during June 1959. However it was not until March 1960 that full equipment was achieved. Most F-86Ls for the 181st FIS had come directly from the 331st FIS at Webb AFB in Texas.

At the start of 1965 the unit converted to the tanker role and replaced the F-86Ls with KC-97Gs. The Sabres, with no other use, had been ferried out to Davis-Monthan by the end of June 1964.

182ND FIGHTER INTERCEPTOR SQUADRON TEXAS ANG

Flying from Kelly AFB, the 182nd FIS converted from F-80Cs to F-86D Sabres in December 1957, equipping with freshly-overhauled aircraft from McClellan AFB. The Sabres were retained until July 1959 when most were reassigned to Puerto Rico and Louisiana ANG units. The 182nd FIS then began to equip with F-86Ls – receiving its first aircraft from the 56th FG at O'Hare AFB in June 1959. All subsequent aircraft for the 182nd FIS came from the 56th FG. The 182nd FIS then became the first ANG F-102A unit in mid-1960, and lost its last F-86L to Davis-Monthan in July of that year.

Below, in August 1957, Maj Bobby Taylor, CO of the 111th, shows off the unit's first Sabre Dog to friends at the 182nd which would receive their first F-86D in December 1957. (Texas ANG via Norm Taylor)

Above, F-86D 51-6249 from the 111th FIS visits the 182nd FIS at Kelly AFB, San Antonio, TX, in 1957. The sign on the World War One vintage hangar in the background reads: "136th Field Maintenance Squadron Texas Air National Guard, Tow Em In, Fly Em Out". (TX ANG via Norm Taylor) At left, 1958 "Summer Camp" on 4 June 1958. Eight 111th F-86Ds in original austere markings which were soon to change. (J. Howard via Mitchell Hail) Below, F-86D 52-3839 with 136Th ADW emblem on the nose belonged to Maj Bobby Taylor, CO of the 111th FIS and is seen in late 1958 at NAS New Orleans where he was visiting the 122nd LA Air Guard. Fuselage and tail stripes were red outlined in white. (TX ANG via Michael Hail)

Above, Operation Pick-Up: on 9 February 1958, members of the 111th FIS were detailed to walk the ramp and do a FOD sweep. The exercise was ordered after Foreign Object Damage was noted during an engine inspection. Note some aircraft have red tail stripes with the squadron insignia added to the tail and three aircraft have canopy covers installed. (T. Densford, SR, TX ANG via Mitchell Hail) Below, F-86L 52-3752 at Ellington AFB had the state of Texas emblem on the left side of the fuselage nose and the 147th FIW emblem on the right side of the fuselage nose. The tail had a red stripe with the 111th FIS emblem on it. (Don Spering A. I. R. collection)

29

Above, 111th FIS F-86Ls in their ADC alert shed at Ellington AFB on 18 October 1959. Aircraft have da-glo fuselage markings outlined in black. (TX ANG via Mitchell Hail) At left, 111th FIS Sabre Dog is guarded by a squadron MP during "Summer Camp" in June 1959 at Ellington AFB. (TX ANG via Mitchell Hail) Below, final pair of 111th FIS F-86Ls left Hensley Field on 20 June 1964. 53-1011 was flown by Maj Tad Foran, at right. Small open hinged access panel in the lower nose area gave access to the rocket package ground test switches. (TX ANG)

111TH FIS

Above, 111th Texas ANG personnel load rockets into the front end of the lowered belly rocket tray in June 1959. Note rocket cart with explosive warning signs parked in front of aircraft. (TX ANG via Mitchell Hail) At right, two 111th armorers, Tanner and Lloyd, load rockets from the rear of the rocket tray at Ellignton AFB on 6 January 1958. (TX ANG via Mitchell Hail) Below, locally designed and produced jet engine test stand used for maintenance of F-86D/L Sabre Dogs in service with the Texas ANG. (TX ANG via Mitchell Hail)

Above, two Texas ANG 181st FIS F-86Ds in 1957, were highlighted with da-glo nose, aft-fuselage band and outer wing panels. Tail stripe was yellow outlined in black with the squadron insignia applied to it. 51-8478 had the 147th FIG insignia on the forward fuselage and 52-3854 had the state of Texas badge applied to its nose. (Densford via Don Spering) Below, F-86D 52-3770 on display at Bergstrom AFB in 1958 had black outlines to its da-glo trim and blue-tipped wing tanks. (TX ANG via Mitchell Hail) Bottom, 181st F-86D 52-3787 on 24 January 1959 had the da-glo markings removed and had its undersides painted aircraft gray. (TX ANG via Mitchell Hail)

181ST FIS

Above, 181st FIS F-86Ls on the squadron's ramp at Hensley Field, NAS Dallas, TX, in July 1964, just prior to their replacement with KC-97 tanker aircraft. (TX ANG via Mitchell Hail) At right, 181st F-86D instrument panel on 5 April 1959 at NAS Dallas. (TX ANG via Mitchell Hail) Bottom, close-up of radar reflector installed under the forward fuselage (see page 16 for an overall photo of an aircraft fitted with a radar reflector) of a 181st FIS F-86D on 29 April 1959 at NAS Dallas. (TX ANG via Mitchell Hail)

Above, 181st F-86L-60 53-1030 became a display aircraft and is seen 6-months after its retirement on 6 January 1965 at Hensley Field. In October 1998 it was moved to Carswell Field, Fort Worth Joint Reserve Base, along with the 181st. (Norm Taylor) At left, 181st crewman fills a Sabre Dog wing tank at NAS Dallas on 24 January 1959. Bottom, 181st FIS F-86L-55 53-694 on 22 June 1963 in the unit's final color scheme which included aircraft gray undersides and the ANG insignia and TEXAS on the tail. (via Norm Taylor)

182ND FIS TEXAS ANG

Above, 182nd FIS F-86D 52-3644 in December 1957 immediately after delivery from the Sacramento Air Depot. The receiving ANG unit just had to apply the state's abbreviation to the fuselage and add squadron and wing markings. (TX ANG via Mitchell Hail) At right, after delivery to the 182nd, a red tail band was added to the tail as well as the squadron insignia. (Kaston) Below, 182nd "scramble", Sgt Peterson holds helmet as Capt Goodman climbs ladder. Capt Heron and TSqt Jimenez run to their aircraft. (USAF)

182ND FIS TEXAS ANG

Above, four da-glo trimmed 182nd FIS F-86Ls in flight out of Kelly AFB, TX, in 1960. (TX ANG via Norm Taylor) At left, BGen Harry Crutcher, commander of the 136th ADW, with Maj Nowell Didear, commander of the 182nd FIS, inspects the honor guard at Summer Camp in 1958 at Kelly AFB, San Antonio, TX. F-86Ds can be seen in the background. (TX ANG via Mitchell Hail) Below, F-86Ds in the alert barn at the 182nd FIS at Kelly AFB, San Antonio, TX, in July 1959. (TX ANG via Mitchell Hail)

191ST FIGHTER INTERCEPTOR SQUADRON UTAH ANG

Based at Salt Lake City Airport, the 191st FIS flew F-86Es until they began to be replaced by F-86Ls in April 1958. Full strength on the F-86L was achieved in March 1959 and coincided with the departure of the last F-86E. The F-86Ls were lost when the unit converted to the cargo role with C-97s in April 1961. The Sabres were all sent to Davis-Monthan in February and March of the same year.

At top, three 191st FIS F-86Ls in flight with 53-997 in the foreground. (UT ANG via Norm Taylor) At right, Utah ANG F-86L 53-955 in May 1959 with ghost markings from its former USAF unit still visible. (via Norm Taylor) Below, 191st F-86Ls 53-813 and 53-997. (UT ANG via Norm Taylor)

At left, 191st FIS F-86L 53-3681 at the Salt Lake City Airport in Utah in 1959 had da-glo trim consisting of a large nose band and rear fuselage band and outer wing panels. (Picciani via Isham)

187TH FIGHTER INTERCEPTOR SQUADRON WYOMING ANG

Operating from Cheyenne Municipal Airport, the 187th FIS converted from F-80Cs to F-86Ls beginning in early March 1958. The F-86Ls were gained mostly from the 456th FIS at Castle AFB and remained for nearly three years. The squadron converted to MC-119s in the aeromedical transport role in February 1961, and the last of the F-86Ls departed for Davis-Monthan in March 1961.

Below, Wyoming ANG 187th FIS F-86L 52-4274 lifts-off from the Cheyenne Municipal Airport in the summer of 1958. It was retired to Davis-Monthan in February 1961. (via Duncan Curtis) Bottom, 187th FIS flight line in May 1959 with F-86L-50 52-10159 in the foreground. The aircraft and its squadron mates were highlighted by da-glo trim. (via Norm Taylor)

38

DENMARK – ROYAL DANISH AIR FORCE/KONGELIGE DANSKE FLYVEVABEN

As a NATO signatory, Denmark started to receive MDAP aid from the USA in the 1950s, comprising 200 or more Thunderjets, and for training use, a few T-33s. The Royal Danish Air Force (RDAF) continued to utilize British-supplied Meteor fighters and interceptors, however.

All that changed in 1958 when Denmark became the second overseas nation to receive the F-86D (just ten days after the Japanese accepted their first Dog.) Under MAP Project 7F-733, thirty-eight ex-USAF F-86D-31 aircraft were ferried into NAA's Inglewood plant during early December 1957 for overhaul. These aircraft were then flown to Brookley AFB in Alabama for preservation in preparation for overseas shipment. One machine, 51-6006, was written off in a flying accident on 26 May 1958 and replaced in the Danish order by another F-86D-31. The aircraft assembled at Brookley would travel to Europe by ship, and on 6 June 1958 they were formally handed over to MAP and loaded aboard the carrier USS *Tripoli* at Mobile.

Upon arrival at the port of Aalborg in Denmark, the coccooned Sabres were offloaded and transferred by road to the nearby Aalborg AB, new home of the RDAF's interceptor force. They were accepted on 26 June 1958 and allowed Eskadrille (Esk) 723 at Aalborg to convert from Meteor NF.11s. Danish pilots had trained at Perrin AFB in Texas during 1957/58, though Perrin had lost most of its F-86Ds by that time and the crews instead received flight training on the F-86L. To support the conversion process, USAF pilots and maintenance crews were attached to the RDAF at Aalborg, and these personnel came from various 86th FIW units in Germany. This small group comprised five pilots and eighteen maintenance personnel. USAF pilots flew the initial test flights on all aicraft as

Above, F-945 (51-5945) shows the later scheme worn by Royal Danish Air Force Sabre Dogs. Danish flag on the tail was red and white. The aircraft served with Esk 723. (Hans Kofoed via Jack Freil)

they were de-preserved by the maintenance crews. Both groups then began teaching the Danish personnel on maintenance and flying of the F-86Ds. The USAF detachment returned to Germany at the end of 1958.

The Sabres initially carried few markings other than the Danish roundel in the usual six positions and a stylised Danish flag on the vertical fin. In order to distinguish different units, code letters were used, painted in large figures on the forward fuselage.

On 28 May 1960, a further batch of seventeen F-86Ds arrived in Denmark aboard the 14,000-ton cargo ship USNS *Marine Fiddler* followed by a further four on 5 August. These aircraft were all ex-USAFE F-86D-36s, and this influx enabled Esk 728 to re-equip.

Aside from the F-86D's troublesome fuel control system, the RDAF found that the aircraft's unguided rocket armament was becoming outdated in the late '50s. The solution came in 1960 when all remaining F-86Ds were modified to use the GAR-8 Sidewinder air-to-air missile (later re-designated AIM-9). This immediately provided the Air Force with a potent interceptor, and also allowed stern intercepts against targets including those at supersonic speeds. The squadrons did, however, discover that at low altitude, the efficiency of the GAR-8 was hampered by ground "clutter" and was not to be considered

a useful weapon below 2,000 ft.

A further change occurred soon after 1960, when most of the Sabres were converted to carry the improved British Martin-Baker Mk.5 ejector seat, along with TACAN navigation equipment. The Danes realized that the original NAA ejector seat included no survival equipment and would give a pilot limited chances if he ejected over water. The subsequent modification of RDAF F-86Ds to receive the Martin Baker Mk5 seat, as well as an effective simulator training program, provided the pilots with the skills required to take proper action and proved its worth immediately. From the time that the Mk.5 seats were modified into the fleet, fifteen ejections were successfully initiated without loss of life, even though one ejection was made with the aircraft in a dive below 400 ft. In another case the pilot spent 50 minutes in near zero-degree water before being rescued. His body temperature was 29 degrees C when he arrived at the hospital and regained consciousness. His first action was to get away from the nurse, whom in his bewildered state he thought to be a Russian interrogator! (she wore red markings on a white cap).

SEMPER VIGILANS

One final delivery of Sabres was made to Denmark: one F-86D-41 and a pair of F-86D-45s which arrived by rail from the USAF's Chateauroux depot during March 1962. These three machines were supplied purely as a source of spare parts for the airworthy Sabres in Denmark.

In the early 'sixties, Danish F-86D units carried out live-firing practice with both 2.75" FFARs and Sidewinder missiles over the Mediterranean from Wheelus AFB in Libya. The aircraft's pulse radar at this time was found to be vulnerable to jamming, which meant that the fire control system could not compute the

firing information. The Sidewinder, however, suffered no such shortcomings, and proved to be very effective against even high-speed targets in clear air mass attacks at altitudes above 50,000ft. From late 1958 to early 1966, the F-86Ds were employed as all-weather air defense fighters and provided a means of policing Danish air space as far east as Bornholm on an around-the-clock basis, irrespective of weather.

Twenty-one Danish F-86Ds were lost in service, including one to a ground accident and four in two mid-air collisions. A significant number of these accidents involved engine fires

Above, fitting formation was set up to demonstrate the arrival of the F-104 to replace Sabres with Esk 723 and Esk 726. Sabres were F-504 with F-473 leading. (Oluf Eriksen) Bottom, 51-5958 was the first F-86D assigned to Esk 723 at Aalborg. It was lost in a crash at Zetten, Holland, on 17 April 1961. (via Norm Taylor)

or automatic fuel control failures. Other than the pilot lost by Esk 723 (detailed below), only one other RDAF airman was killed by a Sabre. On 21 April 1960, MSgt Kurt Kruse Jensen died in a tragic ground accident during one of the Wheelus

deployments. It appears that he had been inadequately briefed on engine running and whilst conducting an engine test was sucked into the intake of an F-86D and killed.

Withdrawal from front line use began in June 1965 when both Esk 723 and 726 at Aalborg converted to F-104G Starfighters. Many of the retired Sabres were retained at Aalborg and other Danish bases, and served on as decoy aircraft. After withdrawal from service many of these decoys were painted in an overall olive drab colour scheme to represent the colors worn by RDAF aircraft in service at the time. The F-86D was officially withdrawn from RDAF use on 31 March 1966.

Esk 723

First RDAF unit to receive F-86Ds, Esk 723 at Aalborg, was allotted Sabres starting in June 1958. The aircraft carried consecutive codes from AB-A to AB-T. Esk 723 was initially commanded by Maj K. S. Pedersen who was replaced by Maj. P. Schrøter in 1959.

The unit lost its first aircraft on 1 December 1958 when 51-6090 (AB-M) of Esk 723 crashed at Hvorup. The aircraft was being flown by a student pilot with another F-86D flying chase. In one of the more bizarre accidents, the pilot of AB-M caught

his flying suit in the canopy lock handle. As the canopy flew off, the student panicked and ejected, thinking that his aircraft was in trouble. Luckily he survived the incident. Incredibly, only one Danish pilot lost his life in a Sabre. On 9 March 1960 Flyverloejtnant II S. G. Malmros (flying 51-6017, AB-K) suffered an unspecified problem over Limfjorden and was forced to eject at very low altitude; his parachute failed to deploy fully and sadly he died of his injuries.

The squadron later participated extensively in a Danish film called

Above, Esk. 723 Sabres lined-up at Aalborg in the early days. Gloster Meteors visible at left were replaced by the F-86Ds. (Oluf Eriksen) Below, handover flight of two Esk 723 Meteor NF. 11s and two F-86Ds. (Oluf Eriksen)

"Jet Pilots" and two further officers commanded the unit: Maj. H. V. Hansen from 1962 to 1965 and Maj. A.C. Larsen from 1965 until the Sabres left Esk 723 service in June 1965. The squadron converted to F-104G Starfighters.

Esk 726

Esk 726 under Maj B. K. S. Weng was the second unit to receive Sabres, having moved from Karup to Aalborg on 10 June 1958 in order to consolidate RDAF Sabres at one base. The squadron had previously flown F-84Gs, and received its first F-86D on 23 August 1958, though Weng was actually the first RDAF pilot to fly the F-86D in his native country. In line with other RDAF aircraft, Esk 726 was allotted squadron codes for its aircraft, ranging from AL-A to AL-T. At about the time that the F-86Ds arrived, Esk 726 formed a four-ship aerobatic team which in 1960 helped to celebrate ten years of the RDAF. The team, named "Phantom Blue", flew aircraft painted with a blue "sunburst" on the tail and red lightning flashes running back from the intake lip. Command of the squadron was handed over to Maj. A. C. Larsen in 1960 and further to Maj. K. Abildskov in 1964, who was the last Esk 726 commander in the Sabre era. The unit converted to F-104G Starfighters in June 1965.

Below, the first F-86D handover ceremony at Esk 726 at Aalborg on 23 August 1958. 51-6037 was coded AL-A and was lost in a crash at Ebeltoft on 29 July 1964. (RDAF via Ericksen) Middle, AL-H (51-6034). (Oluf Erikson) Bottom, Phantom Blue aerobatic team F-123 (51-6123) at Solingen AB, Germany, in April 1961. Tail and wing tank markings were blue and nose flash was red. (Merle Olmsted)

Esk 728

Previously flying F-84Gs from Skrydstrup, the unit received its first Sabres in August and was led briefly by Maj H. J. Corfitzen until Maj. E. P. Schneider took over command in 1961. The squadron aircraft briefly carried code letters in the SI-A to SI-Z range, but late in 1960 the whole RDAF serial number system changed. In future, all F-86Ds would be serialled "F-", followed by the "last three" of the USAF serial number. As space was tight at Aalborg, Esk 728 remained at Skrydstrup. Maj Schneider commanded Esk 728 until 1965 when Capt A. M. Rasmussen took over; the latter became the last RDAF F-86D squadron commander. The final RDAF Sabre loss was F-128 (51-6128), which crashed at Ramstein AB in Germany on 14 April 1965.

Esk 728 reluctantly gave its last Sabre demonstration on 17 March 1966 and disbanded on 31 March, ending Denmark's association with the Sabre. Most of Esk 728's F-86Ds were utilized as static decoy airframes until most were finally dismantled and taken to the Oksbol ranges in the early 1990s. It is worth noting that the last F-86D flight in Denmark was accomplished on 14 May 1966, when F-421 was flown into Vaerloese AB for use at the RDAF Technical Training School.

Below, Esk 728 flightline on 17 March 1966. Third in line, F-421 (51-8421) flew the last Sabre flight on 14 May 1966, when it was transferred to Vaerloese for instructional use. (NJR Hansen via Oluf Eriksen)

FRENCH AIR FORCE

Following the World War II, French industry took some time to recover, and this was especially true in the aircraft manufacturing industries. Thus, to begin rebuilding the French Air Force – the Armée de l'Air – many foreign types were purchased, and in 1951, F-84Gs and T-33 trainers began to arrive from the United States, and later on, F-84Fs and F-100Ds began to equip French squadrons. These machines were supplied under MDAP as France was a NATO member at this point. (France withdrew from NATO in 1966, much to the chagrin of member states, not least the United States).

In the interceptor role, France had planned to deploy the Dassault

Mirage, the prototype of which flew in 1955. However, delays in getting the production Mirage IIIC and Vautour IIN into service saw the Armée de l'Air looking to buy an interim aircraft off the shelf. The F-86K was chosen for this requirement.

Above, 55-4814 was the first F-86K delivered to the French AF. The 13-GA code of EC.1/13 was changed to 13-QA in 1958. (Bernard Chenel)

A new unit was formed to receive these Sabres, 13e Escadre de

EC. 1/13

Chasse Tout Temps (ECTT – All Weather Fighter Wing). The unit was activated on 1 March 1955 at Lahr AB in West Germany under the leadership of Commandant Risso. However, delivery of the first F-86Ks did not begin until some time later, and initially eight T-33s were assigned so that crews could begin blind flying instrument training. To familiarize themselves with the F-86K, five 13e ECTT pilots were also detached to Istrana AB in Italy, while ground personnel were trained by four USAF instructors who set up a Field Training Detachment at Lahr. Finally, in June 1956, two Erco MB-18 flight simulators arrived at Lahr so that flight training could be carried out.

This situation continued until 4 September 1956 when the first of sixty FIAT-built F-86Ks arrived at Lahr, being officially accepted by the French the following day. The delivery of F-86Ks triggered the formation of two Escadrons (squadrons) within 13e ECTT on 1 October; Escadron 1 "Artois" with Commanding Officer Capitaine Fonvielle and Escadron 2

"Alpes" under Capitaine Brisset. In French service, these units were known as EC.1/13 and EC.2/13 respectively, denoting their assignment to 13e ECTT.

By the end of 1956 the unit had flown 189 hours in the F-86K, comprising 196 missions. On 1 April 1957, 13e ECTT moved into a new purpose-built base at Colmar-Mayenheim in France, at this time possessing fifty-three of the planned sixty machines. Delivery was completed in June with the arrival of 55-4816 and -4818 at Colmar.

To differentiate between the two Escadrons, the aircraft were assigned individual codes: EC.1/13 using 13-GA to GZ and EC.2/13 having 13-HA-to HZ. It was decided in late 1958 to change these codes: EC.1/13 changed from "13-G" to "13-Q" and EC.2/13 from "13-H" to "13-P". This

Above, red and white fuselage trim on F-86Ks were an anti-collision measure. 55-4827 of EC. 2/13 still sports short-span wings. (Guido Buhlmann via Steve Miller) Bottom, high-speed taxi of F-86K 13 QC on a busy French airfield with Vantour bombers, Mystere and Ouragan fighter-bombers and B-26 Invaders. 55-4816 was lost in a flying accident on 28 January 1959. (Archives Nicolaou)

only gave fifty-two code permutations, and aircraft that were "spare" took on codes in the "13-SA" range.

Armée de l'Air F-86Ks were immediately involved in NATO exercises, participating in "Counter Punch" in late 1957, followed by "Rebecca" in which 13e ECTT took up a 24-hour alert posture. By the end of 1957, more than 2,000 hours had

EC. 2/13

been flown on the F-86K fleet. This was tempered by the first loss of a French F-86K when on 13 April 1957 55-4842 landed short at Colmar, causing the left undercarriage leg to break Pilot Lt Cavat was uninjured, but the Sabre was uneconomical to repair. A further landing accident on 11 June involved 55-4855, the aircraft running off the runway at Colmar. This time no damage was incurred.

Sadly, the start of 1958 also marked the first and only fatal F-86K accident in French service. On 7 January a radio mechanic was sucked into the intake of a running Sabre and killed. At the end of May 1958, exercise "Full Play" began, to simulate a large-scale attack by atom bombers. F-86Ks were the main adversary and at the end of the exercise on 5 June had flown 174 sorties by day and fifty at night. The concentrated flying schedule was continued when 13e ECTT deployed to Cazaux on 16 June for gunnery practice. The F-86Ks fired at targets trailed by Ouragan and B-26 aircraft.

Training continued. On the night of 3 November 1958, EC.2/13 was just reaching the end of a mass night sortie, and no doubt eager to get back safely on the ground, Lt Hervouet landed wheels-up at Colmar. The crash started a small fire and also blocked the runway, Hervouet managing to jump clear while the fire was put out. However, with the runway blocked, the airborne remainder of the squadron was forced to divert into Lahr, where the night's misfortune was compounded when the nose-wheel of Capt Mayot's F-86K broke on landing. Mayot was uninjured, and fortunately both Sabres, 55-4867 and 4843 respectively, were repaired.

During 1959 all F-86Ks began to be routed through FIAT in Turin for IRAN (Inspect and Repair As Necessary) overhaul and modification of mainplanes to "F-40" specification with extended leading edges and increased span. At about the same time, many French F-86Ks had a long red/white/red band applied to each fuselage side in an effort to increase their visibility in the air. This had a valid purpose; despite the application of these markings, on 28 October 1961, 55-4855 and 55-4867 collided in flight, though both machines and pilots recovered safely to base. Another problem encountered by French F-86Ks was that of engine failure,

Above, French F-86Ks used the last two letters of their squadron code as part of their radio call sign. 55-4839 used F-UHGL. After retirement the aircraft was destroyed with dynamite on 19 March 1964. (Archives Nicolaou) Below, 55-4822 (13. QG) of EC. 1/13 landing at Colmar in December 1961. Aircraft is equipped with long-span wings and Sidewinder launch rails. (Werner Gysin via Steve Miller) Bottom, Lt Brugnoli of EC.1/13 walked away from this landing accident at Colmar on 21 April 1960. The aircraft was repaired to fly another day (Bernard Chenel)

sometimes caused by fuel system faults. This resulted in five crashes, four pilots ejecting successfully, and another surviving the subsequent forced landing.

Further modification began at FIAT in June 1960 with the fitting of Sidewinder missile launch rails, and at least twenty-nine aircraft were eventually converted, starting with 55-4820. This modification extended the useful life of the aircraft, but in

June 1961 at a fighter meet at Colmar, two new Mirage IIICs were unveiled in 13e ECTT markings; the writing was on the wall for the French F-86Ks. But it was not until January 1962 that EC.1/13 relinquished its Sabres, passing them to EC.2/13 to begin Mirage conversion. EC.2/13 then also gave up its F-86Ks in April, but at this time it was decided to form a third Escadron, EC.3/13, to operate the Sabres while the Mirage conversion was completed. EC.3/13 took

over the "13-SA to 13-SZ" code range.

The transfer of a number of French F-86Ks to Italy began in early 1962 with the departure of thirteen aircraft to 51° Aerobrigata on 27 January; a further nine departed on 13 July.

The F-86K remained in service until 4 October 1962 when, their usefulness at an end, they were transferred to USAF control under the terms of MAP. At the beginning of June 1963, fifteen airworthy F-86Ks

At top, 55-4849 of EC. 1.13 with brake chute deployed. (Archives Nicolaou) At left, 55-4868 during take-off roll. The aircraft is preserved to this day at the Ditellandia Air Park in Italy. (Archives Nicolaou) Bottom, 55-4850 was the last French F-86K lost in a flying accident, on 3 August 1962. (Archives Nicolaou)

were transferred to Chateauroux for storage, joining sixteen further F-86Ks already at the base. In March 1964 all these aircraft were destroyed by explosives. Only one aircraft survived in France: 55-4841, which was given to the French and placed on display at the entrance to Colmar AB. It is now proudly displayed in the Musée de l'Air in Paris.

At right and below, 55-4860 shows the right side "hirondelle" badge of EC. 1/13, not often seen on the unit's aircraft. A stylized chimaera appeared on the left fuselage side. Note original short-span wings fitted to this aircraft. (Archives Nicolaou)

GERMAN LUFTWAFFE

Post-war rebuilding of Germany's Luftwaffe began in October 1954, when member states agreed to allow the formation of a new German army, navy and air force. The F-86K was chosen as the air force's all-weather interceptor.

Delivery of eighty-eight F-86Ks from FIAT began in 1957. Arriving at Oberpfaffenhofen from Italy in pairs, the first two (55-4866 and 55-4878) were flown in on 22 July; delivery was completed on 23 June 1958. All these aircraft carried USAF markings for the ferry flight. The Luftwaffe complement of F-86Ks was comprised of forty-three 55-Fiscal Year aircraft and forty-five from 56-FY. The latter were delivered with long-span wings and were thus favored for assignment to front-line units. Very few 55-FY F-86Ks saw service with the Luftwaffe and those that did were fitted with long-span wings at Dornier prior to unit assignment.

Incredibly, the F-86Ks were placed into immediate storage by Dornier, awaiting trained personnel to fly and maintain the aircraft. It was not until WS 10 began training F-86K crews in 1959 that the aircraft were then de-preserved and put into service. Even then, less than sixty of these Sabres saw service, the

remaining machines remained in store, still in their USAF colors.

With the loss of a number of aircraft to flying accidents, the 55-FY Sabres began to be removed from storage in 1962 and approximately ten eventually made their way to Jadgeschwader (fighter wing) 74. In addition to four F-86Ks lost in flying accidents, a number were also written off as a result of engine fires, including 55-4923 and 56-4127 (the latter on 2 April 1962). The remaining components of these two aircraft were later combined and returned to service, gaining serial number 55-4923.

There were never sufficient personnel and aircraft available to equip the two planned wings (Jagdgeschwader) of F-86Ks and thus JG 75 only operated them for a short time before

Above, Luftwaffe F-86Ks were all delivered in USAF colors. 55-4925 arrived at Dornier on 25 November 1957. The aircraft saw service as JD-252 and was later sold to Venezuela as s/n 0028. (Peter Sickinger)

personnel and aircraft were absorbed into JG 74. Despite this the fleet had flown 10,000 hours by 8 April 1963 and reached the 20,000-hour landmark on 23 April 1964.

The F-86K was withdrawn from Luftwaffe service on 31 December 1965 and most of the surviving aircraft and spares were passed to the Venezuelan Air Force. Many of the stored aircraft at Oberpfaffenhofen — still in USAF colors — were also passed to Venezuela.

WAFFENSCHULE 10

In June 1959, about 120 person-

nel, mainly technicians, were posted to Oldenburg to form the first F-86K training unit. On 16 July, 3 Staffel (squadron) of Waffenschule 10 (Weapons School 10 — WS 10) was set up at Oldenburg to begin F-86K training and Hauptmann (Captain) Ulrich Pieper then transferred the unit's first F-86K from

Above, the first F-86K to enter Luftwaffe service was 56-4140. It was coded BB-701 at WS.10, Oldenburg, but later moved to Karlsruhe to continue instructional duties. (Dave Menard)

Oberpfaffenhofen to Oldenburg in August. 3./WS 10 was assigned three F-86Ks by 10 September 1959: 56-4140, 55-4935 and 55-4936. These aircraft were given the unit codes BB-701 to 703, respectively. Concurrent delivery of aircraft for the anticipated front-line units began at this time and flying training under WS 10 tutelage began using these machines. After approximately one year of training the unit was declared sufficiently proficient on the F-86K and 3./WS 10 transformed into Jagdgeschwader 75 in October 1960.

Above, JD-320 3./JG 74 was previously 56-4124. Seen at Neuberg AB in September 1965, just prior to the type's withdrawal from German service. Forward half of drop tank was powder blue, back half white. (S. Peltz via Norm Taylor)

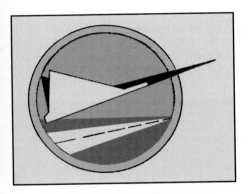

JAGDGESCHWADER 74

Activating at Neuberg/Donau in April 1961, JG 74 was a "paper" re-numbering of JG 75 after personnel shortages dictated that only one Luftwaffe F-86K wing would be formed. JG 74 took over all personnel and aircraft from JG 75.

JG 74 also inherited a few natural metal finished F-86Ks, though the camouflage scheme was quickly standardised on all aircraft. JG 74's unit code was "JD" and this was painted over the existing "JE" code of JG75. On 5 December 1962 JG 74 was assigned to NATO.

Incredibly, during this period no F-86Ks had been lost in flying accidents; this was not to last. On 3 May 1962 two aircraft (56-4119/JD-109 and 56-4133/JD-103) collided on approach to Neuburg. Both pilots, Oberleutnant Alfred Winkelmann and Feldwebel Manfred Haaso, were killed. On 30 October the following year Oberleutnant Klaus Richter was more fortunate; he managed to eject from 56-4130 (JD-101) near Neuburg.

In 1964, JG 74 was alerted for conversion to the F-104G Starfighter, and on 31 March the two original Staffel transferred their remaining aircraft to newly-formed 3 Staffel of JG 74 so that conversion could begin. F-86K aircraft codes were concurrently reapplied in the "JD-331" to "JD-351" range. The final Luftwaffe F-86K accident involved a 3./JG 74 machine — 56-4157 (JD-316)-which crashed near Schwabisch Gmund on 24 November 1964 after an engine explosion. The pilot ejected safely.

Inevitably, with the arrival of F-104Gs, JG 74 began to draw down its F-86K operations and though officially withdrawn from use on 31 December 1965, the final F-86K mission was flown on 5 January 1966. All surviving Sabres were flown to Dornier for overhaul and resale.

Below, JD-249 ex-56-4158 was assigned to 2 Staffel, 2./JG 74 at Neuberg. It was later redesignated JD-349 as part of 3./JG 74 and was eventually sold to Venezuela as s/n 5627. The squadron insignia was applied to the tail and the top of the wing tank was dark green. (via Craig Kaston)

JAGDGESCHWADER 75

With 3./WS 10 reaching readiness on the F-86K, Major Fritz Wegener was assigned to Oldenburg in September 1960 to transform the unit from a training regime to an operational fighter wing; JG 75 began operations in October using personnel and aircraft transferred "on paper" from WS 10. It had been planned to move JG 75 to the new airfield at Neuberg/Donau, but as it was not yet completed, the unit instead moved to Leipheim in October 1960.

JG 75 assigned its aircraft to two individual Staffel (squadrons): 1./JG 75 and 2./JG 75. These squadrons painted the "JE" code of JG 75 in black on the noses of their aircraft, followed by a three-figure individual aircraft number, running from 101 to 128 for 1 Staffel and from 231 to 251 for 2 Staffel. The units flew natural metal finished aircraft for a short time before camouflage markings were applied in late 1960; not all of JG 75's F-86Ks were painted, however.

Finally, in April 1961, JG 75 was able to move into its new base at Neuburg/Donau. However, the unit's tenure was short-lived. On 5 May 1961 General Kammhuber, inspector of the Luftwaffe, announced that because of a shortage of personnel, it was not possible to set up the second F-86K fighter wing; concurrently JG 75 was re-numbered as JG 74. Personnel, equipment and aircraft were transferred to the "new" unit and JG 75 ceased to be.

Above, JD-347 ex-56-4151 3 Staffel, JG 74 at Neuberg in September 1965. It was retired on 31 December 1965 and sold to Venezuela as s/n 1107. (S. Peltz via Norm Taylor) Below, all luftwaffe F-86Ks initially wore natural metal finish. JE-101 of JG 75 was lost in an accident on 3 December 1960. (Peter Sickinger) Bottom, F-86K test equipment was extensive - this setup was used to test the fire control system. 56-4142 was coded JE-240 and assigned to 2/JG 75. (Peter Sickinger)

GREECE AIR FORCE
ELLINIKI AEROPORIA

The Greek Air Force (Elliniki Aeroporia) operated F-86Ds for only a short period gaining 36 F-86D-36s and a single F-86D-50 in 1960. The previous year these aircraft had been routed into the FIAT overhaul facility at Turin-Caselle, many coming from storage at Chateauroux in France. All were ex-USAFE.

Following overhaul, the first batch of F-86Ds arrived in Greece on 17 May 1960, having been handed-over to the Greek Air Force at Turin on the same day. They were flown into Greece by pilots of 112 Combat Wing, which would go on to form the first F-86D squadron.

The transition from F-86Es to F-86Ds was very smooth, many Greek pilots considering that the F-86D was easier to fly than the E model. The F-86D was the first jet in Greek AF ser-

vice that did not have machine gun or cannon armament; it was also the first that had radar. Training was made in close co-operation with "Mambo" ground radar located on Mount Parnitha. Greek F-86D operations ceased in May 1967. Towards the end of their flying service, a number of Greek F-86Ds were painted in a camouflage scheme. Still in these colors, they were then used as decoy aircraft at a number of air bases until the early 1990s.

Above, Greek F-86D-36 shows key elements of Sabre Dogs supplied under MAP. TACAN antenna on the nose, rear fuselage "sugar scoop" intakes and Sidewinder launch rails. (Themis Vranas) Below, the 337th insignia was painted prominately on the tail of this F-86D-36. Note the rocket cart in the foreground with four Sidewinders to be loaded on Greek Sabre Dogs. (Themis Vranas) Bottom, a number of 337 Mira F-86Ds were camouflaged in later service, 51-6171 is in the foreground. (Themis Vranas)

337 Mira

The first Greek F-86D unit to equip was 337 Mira Anaghetiseos Pantos Kerou (MAPK - all weather interceptor squadron) at Elefsina in the summer of 1960. Coming under 112 Combat Wing control, 337 MAPK was initially commanded by LtCol Economou. Prior to receiving Sabres, the unit had operated as a fighter-bomber squadron with F-84G Thunderjets.

The initial 25 pilots of 337 MAPK were all F-86E veterans, coming from the three existing Greek day fighter

Sabre squadrons - 341, 342, and 343 Mira. Later, another eight Second Lieutenants, trained by the USAF, were posted to the squadron.

In November 1966 the unit was transferred to 111 CW control and began conversion to the Northrop F-5A/B. The last 337 MAPK F-86Ds were withdrawn in May 1967. One source indicates that 6-7 F-86Ds were kept operational with 114 CW at Tanagra until 1969, when the first F-102As arrived in Greece.

Above, after retirement, many F-86Ds were used as "decoy" aircraft on Greek air-fields. 51-5234 still survived at Agrinio in June 1996. Aircraft were brown and green. (Themis Vranas) Below, 51-6179 wears full 343 Mira colors. Tail fin was green and fuselage stripes were yellow and black. (Themis Vranas)

343 Mira

On 12 May 1961, a nucleus of 337 MAPK pilots was embodied into 343 MAPK at Nea Anghialos and took over the transition of squadron pilots to the F-86D. 343 MAPK had previously flown the F-86E and was assigned to 111 CW control. The first CO of 343 MAPK as an F-86D unit was Maj G Gikopoulos. On 24 February 1961, Maj Nikolaos Kouris took over control; he subsequently became Greek AF Chief of Staff , General HQ of National Defense chief of staff and Under Secretary of State for National Defense.

Only one fatal accident occurred during Greek F-86D operations. On 24 July 1961, Capt Nikolaos Tirovolas was fatally injured when his F-86D crashed near Nea Anghialos. He was taken to Hippokration Hospital in Athens where he died five days later as a result of his serious burns. Tirovolas was one of the original 337 Mira pilots posted-in to begin 343 Mira F-86D operations.

Although 343 was the second unit to receive the F-86D, it was the first to lose them, in November 1965, when they began receiving the F-5A/B Freedom Fighter.

HONDURAS AIR FORCE
FUERZA AÉREA
HONDUREÑA

In 1974, four F-86K all-weather fighters were presented to the Fuerza Aerea Hondurena (FAH – Honduran Air Force) by the Venezuelan govern-

At right, the four FAH F-86Ks were nat-ural metal with a red and white shark-mouth on the nose outlined in black. The tail had the pale blue and white Honduras insignia and FAH and s/n 1101. (Paul Holsen III)

ment. These were assigned to Escuadrilla de Caza-Bombardeo (simply, "fighter bomber squadron") at Base Aérea Coronel Héctor Caracciolo Moncada, La Ceiba. The F-86Ks carried natural metal finish throughout their short service life, and all had bold sharkmouths painted aft of the engine intake. They were given the FAH serials 1100 to 1104.

It is not known when the Honduran F-86Ks were retired; it can only be presumed that their complexity and limited numbers precluded all but the briefest of operational use. Limited maintenance support had come from Venezuela.

Two of the F-86Ks (1100/55-4882 and 1101/55-4899) were advertised for sale by Dumond International, Inc., of Downers Grove, Illinois, during 1984. The airframes had just over 1,000 hours each, but did not sell.

ITALIAN AIR FORCE AERONAUTICA MILITARE ITALIANA

The first official delivery of F-86Ks to the Aeronautica Militare Italiana (Italian Air Force – AMI) was made on 25 July 1955 at Caselle-Nord, in the presence of Italian officials from 1a Regione Aerea di Milano (1st Air Region of Milan). Handover was made by Mrs. Clara Light, US ambassador to Italy, who symbolically transferred seven F-86Ks to the AMI. Actual delivery to the operational units took some time longer, however. FIAT eventually delivered sixty-three F-86Ks directly to the AMI, the last being on 31 October 1957. Sabres for the Italian military were serialled from MM 6185 to MM 6237 (fifty-three aircraft). The final ten F-86Ks of Italy's main order did not receive "MM" numbers. Further examples were obtained from France, which passed twenty-two F-86Ks to 51° Aerobrigata, starting in January 1962 and the Netherlands transfered a further eight for a total of ninety-three. In AMI service, the F-86K became known as "Kappone", a double-play on words, meaning either "Big K" or "capon".

In July of 1957, on orders from the Italian Air Ministry, the serial numbers of AMI F-86Ks changed over from the Italian Matricola Militare (MM) system to original USAF serial number. From that point on, the USAF fiscal year serial numbers were applied to all F-86Ks.

In March 1959, F-86L wings began to be installed on AMI's F-86K fleet, the work being carried out by FIAT. The following year, Aero 3B pylons for Sidewinder missiles were also fitted to the longer-winged machines. In 1966, as a result of accidents involving wing failure, and in

Above, the first Italian-built Fiat F-86K being prepared for its maiden flight at Turin on 23 May 1955. In the cockpit is Col Arthur De Bolt, official representative of North American Aviation in Italy. (Boeing)

response to a 1964 Technical Order pertaining to F-86F center sections, FIAT completed the structural strengthening of outer wings and fuselage center sections on AMI F-86Ks. Concurrently, new limits were

Though the last AMI F-86K mission was flown on 27 July 1973, the type was officially withdrawn on 31 July. In Italian service, the F-86Ks had flown 162,396 hours.

At top, MM6185 (53-8273) was the first Italian F-86K. Seen shortly after its first flight of 23 May 1955, it was lost in a landing accident on 24 February 1960 while assigned to 22 Gruppo. The pilot, Loris Barbieri was killed. (Archives Nicolaou) At left, still bearing traces of former French AF markings, 55-4837 was one of a number which received strengthened center sections at Fiat. It is seen at the Turin-Caselle plant shortly after roll-out on 8 June 1966. Note addition of Aero 3B Sidewinder launch rails. (Jack Friell)

1 STORMO

Above, 6° Gruppo was the first Italian F-86K unit. MM6218 (53-8306) was later re-coded 1-07. Tail band was red with 1° Stormo insignia applied over it. (JMG Gradidge)

6° Gruppo COT

To receive the first F-86Ks, 6° Gruppo C.O.T. (Caccia Ogni Tempo - All-Weather Fighter) was formed at Treviso's Istrana AB in October 1955. However, the first pair of F-86Ks – MM 6192 and MM 6193 – didn't arrive there until 2 November. They were flown from Turin by Capitano Fulvio Ristori and Capitano Aldo Scerna. Two days later a third aircraft was delivered and on 19 November three others arrived. By the end of the year 6° Gruppo had received eleven F-86Ks, the final three arriving on 23 December. Each Italian Gruppo was equivalent in size to a USAF squadron, and 6° Gruppo was assigned to the reconstituted 1° Stormo Caccia Interccetori (Fighter Interceptor Group).

6° Gruppo under Maggiore (major) Carlo Tomassi immediately began its conversion to the new aircraft and among the first pilots to fly the F-86K were Squadriglie (flight) Commanders Capitano Fulvio Ristori and Aldo Scerna, respective commanders of 79 and 81 Squadriglie. In its first month of operation 6° Gruppo flew 23 hours and 30 minutes under the guidance of two USAF pilots, Maj Owens and Capt Bruce Ferguson. Into 1956, further deliveries were made to 6° Gruppo, so that at the end of August 1956 the unit had forty-two aircraft. This large number was held in anticipation of the formation of further Gruppi. Despite the profusion of aircraft, 6° Gruppo only achieved 1904 flight hours for the year, a result of spares shortages and periodic groundings for completion of Technical Order modifications.

Once the unit had settled down to a representative twenty aircraft, 6°

Gruppo's Sabres carried nose codes in the 1-01 to 1-21 range. The 1° Stormo badge was painted on the vertical against a red band.

The unit experienced the first AMI F-86K loss on 20 April 1956. Two aircraft, piloted by Capitano Adolfo Shenert and USAF Capt Bruce Ferguson, left Istrana at 1410hrs and soon afterwards Shenert's Sabre, 53-8303 (MM 6215), disintegrated following an explosion. The pilot, one of the unit's more experienced flyers, died in the crash. He had been alerted to a serious engine fire by Capt Ferguson and had intended to try an emergency landing on the runway at Istrana against the departure direction. Though Capt Ferguson had radioed Shenert to eject, he only flew for a short time before his aircraft exploded. The fragmentary nature of the wreckage made it difficult to determine a cause for this accident, other than that it had resulted from a fire in the engine's hot section, which had already taken hold during the take-off run.

On 1 March 1958 the unit lost a further Sabre when the aircraft of Capitano Sebastiano Licheri and Tenente Mazzerelli collided in flight near Treviso. Licheri was forced to eject and landed safely; his Sabre (53-8317) exploded when it hit the ground. Ten Mazzerelli managed to recover to Istrana, but his Sabre (55-4892) sported a large hole in its fin.

On 1 May 1959 6° Gruppo became a guided missile unit, and the F-86Ks were transferred to 22° Gruppo at Istrana.

12° Gruppo

12° Gruppo converted from Canadair Sabre 4s to F-86Ks gained from 21° Gruppo in September 1963 at Grosetto and was placed under 4a Aerobrigata control. The squadron commander was Maggiore Vasco Lucci.

On 19 September the unit moved to Gioia del Colle. Aircraft markings were fairly muted, with the famous 4a AB "cavallino rampante" painted on the tail fin in black against a white cloud formation.

The unit was reassigned to the newly-formed 36° Stormo on 1 August 1966 and concurrently gained a colorful set of markings. On the fin, three green triangles formed a "sawtooth" design, outlined in white. Over this was painted the 36° Stormo badge.

One of the most baffling incidents to affect the AMI Sabre fleet occurred on 28 August 1967. Gruppo Commander Maggiore Corrado Bassi left Gioia on a night flight just after 8

Below, when 12° Gruppo transferred to 36° Stormo control its aircraft gained more colorful markings comprising a green "sawtooth" pattern on the tail fin. This was usually outlined in white. Tail badge was that of 36° Stormo and the fuselage badge is that of ECTT 2/30, a French AF unit, unofficially applied during a squadron visit to RAF Luqa on Malta during 1967. (via Norm Taylor)

o'clock, and somehow became incapacitated. His F-86K, apparently on autopilot, flew on until it eventually ran out of fuel. The aircraft (55-4859) was later found near Manfredonia; it had crashed at approximately 2330hrs.

In December 1971, 12° Gruppo also converted to the Starfighter, and any viable F-86Ks were ceded to the only AMI Sabre unit remaining: 23° Gruppo at Rimini-Miramare.

17° Gruppo COT

The second AMI F-86K unit was 17° Gruppo, constituted under 1° Stormo on 1 May 1956. Commanded by Maggiore Francisco Fatigati, 17° Gruppo immediately received eighteen F-86Ks from 6° Gruppo, both squadrons operating from Istrana. 17° Gruppo possessed three flights: 56, 72 and 80 Squadriglie. Aircraft from the Gruppo were coded in the 1-31 to 1-51 range, and the 1° Stormo badge was painted on the vertical tail

Above, another 12° Gruppo aircraft 55-4865 at RAF Luqa, Malta, during 1967. 36° Stromo insignia is on the tail. Pilot's parachute hangs from the Sidewinder launch rail, and his helmet sits on the wing above it. (D. Goodman via Norm Taylor)

against a blue band.

With transfer of 1° Stormo to guided missile operations on 1 May 1959, 17° transferred its Sabres to 21° Gruppo.

51° Aerodriglie

21° Gruppo COT

Previously flying F-84Fs at Istrana, 21° Gruppo converted to the F-86K in May 1959, gaining ex-17° Gruppo aircraft. It was commanded by Maggiore Antonio D'Alessio and assigned to 51° Aerobrigata control, remaining at Istrana. 21° Gruppo had four flights of F-86Ks, comprising 351, 386, 387 and 388 Squadriglie. The unit applied a 51° Aerobrigata badge to vertical tail of its aircraft,

superimposed against a blue band.

The unit lost its first F-86K on 12 April 1960 when 53-8277, piloted by Tenente Bruno Nardini, exploded and crashed on the plains of Scaltanigo near Treviso. The pilot managed to eject and landed safely near Santa Maria de Sala.

21° Gruppo converted to the F-104G in September 1963, passing its F-86Ks to 12° Gruppo.

22° Gruppo COT

Istrana-based 22° Gruppo converted from F-84Fs in May 1959, gaining ex-6° Gruppo F-86Ks. 22° Gruppo remained assigned to 51° Aerobrigata control at Istrana and was commanded by Maggiore Pierluigi Piccio, who transferred from 6° Gruppo. Like its sister unit, 22° Gruppo comprised four individual flights – 352, 353, 354 and 355 Squadriglie. 22° Gruppo F-86Ks car-

ried a 51° Aerobrigata badge on the vertical tail of its aircraft, applied against a red band.

On 24 February 1960, the squadron suffered a tragic blow when Tenente Loris Barberi, flying 53-8273, was killed on a night interception training mission. Just as the aircraft were returning to land, and at approximately one mile from the runway, his aircraft suddenly dropped from the glide path. Despite calls from the radar controller, the aircraft continued to descend and, 400 meters from the runway threshold, crashed into a house, destroying it. In the rubble and wreckage rescue crews found not only the body of the pilot, but also of a young peasant and some cows.

With F-104S deliveries begin-

Above, 53-8316 wears the red tail band of 22° Gruppo, based at Istrana. Formerly serialled MM 6228, it was originally delivered to 6° Gruppo on 14 June 1956.

ning, 22° Gruppo moved to Cameri on 9 June 1969 for conversion to the type, passing its remaining Sabres to 12° and 23° Gruppi.

23° Gruppo COT

On 1 December 1956, a third F-86K unit was formed within 1° Stormo – initially as Sezione (flight) of 1∞ Stormo, but re-named as 23° Gruppo on 30 March 1957. 6° and 17° Gruppi immediately reassigned aircraft to the

Sezione, and the unit started operations with twelve F-86Ks. Commanded by Capitan Fulvio Ristori, it immediately moved out to Pisa San Giusto as it was unable to operate from Istrana; aside from two

Above, longest-serving of all AMI Sabre units, 23° Gruppo flew the F-86K for more than sixteen years. The tail stripe beneth the 51° Stormo insignia was yellow. 55-4815 was a former French AF aircraft. (Jack Friell)

At left, the 23° Gruppo F-86K was visiting the RAF base at Luqa, Malta, in 1967. The tail insignia and nose codes indicate the unit's assignment to 51° Aerobrigata. (via Norm Taylor) Bottom, final color scheme for Italian F-86Ks was worn by 23° Gruppo machines when they transferred to 5° Stormo in 1973. The "5-" nose code, signifying 5° Stormo, was only worn for four months. (via Mick Roth)

Gruppi of F-86Ks, the base was also home to 21° and 22° Gruppi with F-84F Thunderstreaks. Once given full squadron status, 23° Gruppo had two Squadriglie assigned: 70 and 71 and command of the unit was transferred to Maggiore Francesco Terzani.

23° Gruppo applied squadron codes to its aircraft in the 1-61 to 1-79 range. The 1° Stormo badge was painted on the vertical against a yellow band.

When the units of 1∞ Stormo converted to Nike Ajax guided missiles in May 1959, 23° Gruppo remained an F-86K unit, but was reassigned to 51° Aerobrigata control. The Aerobrigata (air brigade) was similar in size to the standard three-squadron USAF group/wing. 23° Gruppo retained its yellow tail band, but replaced the 1° Stormo badge with that of 51° Aerobrigata.

23° Gruppo moved to Rimini-Miramare in July 1964 and experienced a number of accidents at its new base; thankfully most ended safely. In the evening of 17 February 1966, soon after take-off, Capitano Alberto Frigo's Sabre hit a reinforced concrete pole supporting high tension cables. Capt. Frigo had just retracted the undercarriage and flaps; his attention was momentarily distracted and it was then that he hit the top of the pole. It struck the Sabre's left wing and immediately wrenched off the drop tank on that side; the leading-edge slats were also heavily damaged. The aircraft banked sharply to the left and although only a few feet above the ground, Frigo managed to regain control and ask the control tower for immediate landing clearance. He then succeeded in accelerating to 200 kt and climbed to 2,000 feet. Realizing that the aircraft was still stable he performed stall checks and elected to land; incredibly Frigo recovered the aircraft, s/n 53-8276, safely to base. The concrete pole was later measured; it originally stood 7.20 meters high and after collision was cut down to a height of 4.20 meters.

While considerable effort was being expended on serious problems with structural integrity, on 13 December 1966 F-86K 55-4854, piloted by Sottotenente (2/Lt) Roberto Campacci, lost its wings after an abrupt pull-up maneuver. The pilot was killed in the accident, which occurred 2 miles south-east of Nocera Umbra.

With inevitable conversion to the F-104 in sight, 23° Gruppo was assigned to 5° Stormo on 25 March 1973, having received its first F-104S on 19 March. With transfer to its new parent, 23° Gruppo retained the yellow tail band, replacing the old insignia with the archer of 5° Stormo. Final unit commander was Tenente Colonel (Lt Col) Alberto Frigo, who as a Capitano in 1966 had been the pilot who flew into a concrete pole.

On 27 July 1973, the last AMI Sabre, 53-8291, coded 5-52 carried out seven flights to mark the withdrawal of the type from service. Seven different pilots managed to fly the aircraft that day, culminating in the final sortie by Capt Mario Pinna, Chief of Operations with 23° Gruppo. He left Rimini at ten minutes past four in the afternoon for the final 50-minute flight of an AMI F-86K.

JAPANESE AIR SELF DEFENSE FORCE

Following WWII, Japan was denied the formation of any military service until 1954. Even then, the new Japanese fighting force was to be used only in a purely defensive role, a situation that exists to the present day. A Japanese Self Defense Law was passed on 2 June 1954, and this was followed by the formation of an air arm, the Japanese Air Self Defense Force (JASDF) on 1 July. Among the aircraft planned for the JASDF, it was hoped to procure 150 F-86Ds to equip two all-weather interceptor wings, each with three squadrons in a pure air defense role. This plan required some modification before it was put into action.

In preparation for the arrival of F-86Ds, on 27 January 1958 JASDF sent twelve pilots to USAF F-86D squadrons in Japan to begin their conversion training. On 19 April the first ground crew personnel were sent to the same units – 4th FIS at Misawa, 40th FIS at Yokota and the 68th FIS at Itazuke – to start their ground courses. The Japanese pilots immediately faced a new challenge – the need to speak English on all training missions; 20 further Japanese pilots left for the United States on 14 May and were trained at Perrin AFB. Once F-86Ds began arriving with the JASDF, the first squadron to form (101st Hikotai) took over the training mission. Maintenance training for the type was concurrently started at the 1st Technical School, Hamamatsu.

On 16 January 1958, three F-86D-36s and an F-86D-50 were handed over to the JASDF from USAF units in Japan. Following overhaul at Tachikawa these aircraft, 51-8368, 51-8344, 51-8375 and 52-4042, were given JASDF serial numbers 84-8101, 84-8102, 84-8103 and 84-8104, respectively. In the Japanese system, the first digit of the serial number related to the year in which the aircraft were delivered – in this case '8' signified 1958.

However no further deliveries were made for some time. Unlike many Far East air forces, Japan's next batch of F-86Ds came from the continental United States, rather than from USAF units in the Pacific region. During late 1957, 11 F-86D-26 and 44 F-86D-31 aircraft were removed from storage at Davis Monthan AFB and ferried to the North American plant at Inglewood in California. Thoroughly overhauled, the Sabres then began to emerge from the maintenance process and were handed over to MAP under Project Number 7F732 from 14 May 1958. The aircraft were then shipped to Japan as deck cargo and the first examples were officially handed over on 6 June. JASDF serial numbers were allotted consecutively from the first four aircraft, this batch receiving serial numbers from 84-8105 to 84-8159, inclusive. Some of the intervening serial numbers were prefixed "94-", however, as a few of the F-86Ds were not accepted until 1959.

The first Japanese F-86D unit to form was 101st Hikotai (squadron), which activated on 1 August 1958 under 3rd Kokudan (wing). The remaining F-86Ds for JASDF all came from USAF units in the Far East, most being overhauled by Shin Meiwa at Komaki or by the maintenance set-up at Tachikawa prior to delivery. This final group of aircraft comprised 14 F-86D-36 and 49 F-86D-45. Handover began in December 1959 and was completed in March 1961; the aircraft were given JASDF serials from 94-8160 to 14-8222 inclusive. Unfortunately, spares

support for the F-86D was stopped on 30 June 1960 and only 98 F-86Ds out of 122 received were actually put into service; the remaining 24 aircraft were reclaimed for spare parts. Nonetheless, in the latter days of JASDF service, only 30% of aircraft were airworthy at any time.

Starting in February 1961, annual three-day weapons meets were held at Komaki AB; further meets were held up to 25 September 1967 when the final gathering took place. In 1964, the JASDF began to apply popular names to its aircraft; under this system, the F-86D was known as 'Gekko' (moonlight). However, the aircraft had only a few years ahead of it. JASDF Headquarters had initially planned to withdraw the F-86Ds from service during 1967, and suspend all repair and overhaul during the 1965 Fiscal Year. However, the phase-out was staggered, the first two units disbanding in December 1967, followed by the final pair in October 1968. In the interceptor role, F-104J Starfighters took over from the F-86Ds, and conversion training began in 1963. On 25 August that year an F-86D from 3rd Kokudan crashed while carrying out an F-104J conversion mission. Maj. Jun Ozaki was killed.

101ST HIKOTAI

The 101st Hikotai was the first JASDF F-86D unit to equip, activating on 1 August 1958 under 3rd Kokudan at Gifu, AB; it served as a training unit for JASDF F-86D pilots, moving to Komaki AB on 6 October. The unit lost its first Sabre on 20 January 1959 when 84-8155 (USAF 51-5857) crashed. On 16 March 1960 another aircraft, 94-8137 (USAF 51-5894) collided with a DC-3 while taxing for the night training mission and was written off. The 101st Hikotai disbanded on 1 October 1968.

The three squadrons of the 3rd Kokudan each wore the golden stylized shachihoko of Nagoya Castle applied over three horizontal red stripes (signifying 3rd Kokudan). In 1963 the 3rd Kokudan markings changed and the three stripes were deleted. In their place, a red sylized shachihoko was painted, under which each squadron applied a colored

Above, 101sqn. 3rd Wing F-86D-31 84-8128 (51-5989) at Yokota AB on 19 May 1963. In early 1963, 3rd Wing aircraft received new tail markings. All had a red shachihoko with a color squadron stripe below: green for 101sqn., yellow for 102sqn., and blue for 105sqn. (T. Matsuzaki)

band - green for 101st Hikotai.

102ND HIKOTAI

Under 3rd Kokudan control, the 102nd Hikotai formed on 1 March 1959 at Komaki. With two squadrons operational the 3rd Kokudan was able to initiate its alert role on 1 September 1959. The unit disbanded on 1

December 1967.

As with the other 3rd Kokudan units, the 102nd Hikotai wore the golden shachihoko and red tail stripes described for the 101st Hikotai. In 1963 the three stripes were deleted and the 102nd Hikotai painted a yellow band below the red shachihoko.

Above, F-86D-31 04-8197 (52-4071) landing at Komaki AB on 28 March 1962. Up until early 1963, 3rd Wing aircraft all had a yellow shachihoko with three red stripes signifying the 3rd Wing. After early 1963, the different squadron's identity was ascertained by the color of the aircraft's tail stripe. (T. Matsuzaki)

At right, yellow stripe on tail of this F-86D identifies it as a 102nd Hikotai machine. Red "schachihoko" stylized "ore" or killer whale was common to all 3rd kokudan aircraft from 1963 on. (via D. Curtis) Below right, 04-8191 (52-10001) at Misawa AB in 1964. The two pale blue stripes outlined in white were worn by the 103rd Hikotai. (Dave Menard) Bottom, F-86D-45 04-8197 at Hyakuri AB on 3 November 1968 was assigned to the 2nd Wing 103rd Hikotai. TACAN antenna is installed on nose aft of radome. (T. Matsuzaki)

103RD HIKOTAI

The 103rd Hikotai was initially formed on 1 March 1960 under 3rd Kokudan control at Komaki. However on 29 May 1961, the unit ended its alert role at Komaki and on 10 June was reassigned to 2nd Kokudan control at Chitose AB. The 103rd Hikotai replaced the 4th Hikotai at Chitose, the latter reassigning its F-86Fs to Komatsu. The F-86D unit was able to resume its alert role at Chitose on 7 August 1961.

The 103rd Hikotai set an enviable record for aircraft in-commission – far exceeding that of the other three F-86D squadrons. The 103rd Hikotai ended its alert role on 7 June 1968, having completed 306 "hot" scrambles. The unit disbanded on 1 October 1968.

103rd Hikotai aircraft wore two blue horizontal tail bands and a stylized representation for the Japanese figure "2" (for 2nd Kokudan).

105TH HIKOTAI

The final unit to come under 3rd Kokudan control was the 105th Hikotai; it was the last JASDF F-86D unit to form, activating on 15 March 1962 at Komaki AB. The 105th Hikotai disbanded on 1 December 1967.

As with the other two F-86D units within the 3rd Kokudan, the 105th Hikotai wore the golden shachihoko and three red striped tail until 1963

when the stripes were deleted. The 105th Hikotai identified its aircraft by applying a blue stripe below the shachihoko design.

Below, 3rd Wing F-86D-31 84-8132 (51-6066) on 21 May 1961 during Armed Forces Day at Yokota AB. (T. Matsuzaki) Bottom, 3rd Wing F-86D-36 04-8166 (51-6214) landing at Komaki AB on 29 March 1963. The "shachi-hoko" on the tail has all but been removed in preparation of receiving new markings. (T. Matsuzaki)

KOREA

Following the end of the Korean War, many USAF units remained in South Korea to counter any further aggression from the North. Among these units were the Sabre-equipped 4th FIW, 8th FBW, 18th FBW, 51st FIW and 58th FBW. However, many of these Wings moved out during 1954, leaving just the 58th FBW at Osan-Ni. Though USAF units did remain in the country after that, they were all rotational in nature and no permanently-stationed USAF fighter squadrons remained by the late 1950s.

The Republic of Korea Air Force (RoKAF) was therefore charged with the air defense of the country, despite the massive RoK Army budget, which left the air force with little money to procure new equipment. Nonetheless in line with many other Far East nations, South Korea was given all-weather interceptor capability with the advent of MAP-supplied F-86Ds.

To begin flying these aircraft, prospective pilots were trained on the new type by USAF personnel. Once the type was established in air force use, new pilots went through the standard RoKAF training curriculum, beginning with T-6s at Sach'on, then on to T-33s with the 16th Basic Training Sqn at Taegu. Advanced Sabre conversion took place with the

F-86Fs of the 17th Advanced Training Sqn at Taegu, and F-86D conversion was undertaken by the squadron at Suwon. Maintenance personnel were likewise initially trained by USAF personnel, but thereafter the technical training was centered on the RoKAF unit at Taejon. In-depth maintenance for the F-86Ds and J47 engines was set up at overhaul sites in Taiwan and Japan, but from 1961 a purpose-built complex was built on the northeast side of Taegu AB and major maintenance of F-86Ds was transferred there. The arrival of the F-86Ds coincided with a major upgrade of the RoKAF infrastructure, not least of which was the formation of Air Combat Command under Brigadier Kim Sung Yong; prior to this all operational units had nominally come under command of the US Air Force's 314th Air Division.

Late in 1959 the first of thirty-two ex-USAF F-86Ds were routed into the

Above, 52-10011, an F-86D-50 of the 109th FS, ROKAF had heavily-weathered tail markings comprised of a yellow lightning bolt over a red tail band. Aircraft has a red nose stripe and is equipped with Sidewinder rocket rails. (via Malcolm Lowe) Below, seen at Suwan AB on 8 May 1968, Sidewinder-equipped F-86D-50 s/n 52-9985 wears the colors of the 108th FS. Upper tail chevron was blue and lower was red. (via Norm Taylor)

Shin Meiwa overhaul facility at Komaki in Japan. Slated for the RoKAF, these aircraft were all F-86D-36 and D-50 models and Shin Meiwa also fitted Aero 3B Sidewinder launch rails to the Sabres. Delivery began in January 1960 and initially enabled one fighter squadron to begin equipping.

The First RoKAF unit to receive F-86Ds was the 108th Fighter Squadron at Suwon, the old USAF

At left, Korean AF F-86D-35 51-8424 preserved along with a B-29 on 26 December 1975. (via Craig Kaston)

base near the west coast. The 108th FS was one of three Sabre units formed under the 10th Fighter Wing, the other pair – 102nd and 103rd FS flying F-86Fs. The wing was commanded by Col Kim Kung Sung. In the summer of 1961 Col. Kim was killed in an air crash and replaced by Col Yoon Eung Yul.

Further deliveries of F-86Ds allowed a second unit to equip under the 10th Fighter Wing in the autumn of 1961. This new squadron, the

109th FS, operated alongside the 108th FS at Suwon. It appears that further attrition deliveries of Sabres were made to Korea, probably coincidental with the withdrawal of F-86Ds in Taiwan during 1966.

Tactical control of both F-86D units centered on a Ground Controlled Intercept (GCI) system similar to that in use by other Sabre Dog operators around the world. However the Korean radar web was compromised by the lack of sites, with

only three covering the northern border with North Korea. On the western side, a radar dish on Paengnyong-do 12 miles off the coast gave good coverage, as did a second site south of Suwon. In the east, however, a single site on the coast at Kangnun was badly shielded by the central mountain range. Thankfully, it was never required to direct F-86Ds in a hostile scenario.

Nonetheless, the Korean peninsula was still a hotspot during the 1960s, typified by the loss of a 10th FW F-86D on 14 January 1964. 52-10031 was shot down by the North Koreans near Panmunjom.

On 30 April 1965, the RoKAF received its first Northrop F-5A at Suwon. It was planned that these aircraft would supplant and eventually replace the Sabres. During the 1978/9 period the last eighteen F-86Ds were finally retired.

NETHERLANDS
KONINKLIJKE LUCHTMACHT
(ROYAL AIRFORCE)

The initial jet fighters assigned to the Koninklijke Luchtmacht (Royal Airforce – KLU) were Gloster Meteor F.8 fighters and Republic F-84G fighter bombers, the latter marking the arrival of the first MDAP-funded aircraft. In 1954, the all-weather requirement was filled with the decision to equip the KLU with F-86K Sabres. This proved to be a controversial move; many high-ranking politicians and air force officers had expected a two-seat machine to be chosen. As late as August 1955, navigators still were being trained in anticipation of the arrival of two-seat interceptors.

The first fifteen NAA-built F-86Ks arrived in Holland on 1 October 1955 aboard the USS Tripoli, and a further eight had been received by the end of the year. Following their assembly

and test flights, the first two KLU Sabres were accepted by 702 Sqn on 8 December. In total, fifty-six NAA-built F-86Ks were assigned to the Dutch AF, completing delivery in April 1957. A further six FIAT-built examples were accepted in April and May of that year, falling somewhat short of being able to fulfill the ideal 25-aircraft squadron strength. Squadron assignment was roughly nineteen F-86Ks for 700 and 701 Sqns. 702 Sqn was officially established as the F-86K operational conversion unit on 1

Above, prior to unit assignment, KLU F-86Ks wore just the national insignia and a small serial number (in this case 54-1278) above the fin insignia. Below the insignia was the KLU code (Q-278). This aircraft entered service on 8 December 1955. (via Craig Kaston)

January 1957. The unit's average strength was sixteen machines. During 1959, KLU Sabre operations were consolidated at Twenthe with

Above, 700 Sqn F-86K Q-283 (54-1283) wears the unit badge on its tail fin against a red background. (via Norm Taylor) Below, formation of 700 Sqn F-86Ks in the early '60s. 54-1255/Q-255 was lost in a crash on 7 May 1963, along with 54-1308. (Archives Nicolaou)

---

the arrival of 700 Sqn from Soesterburg.

In the early '60s, the squadron code system was changed so that all F-86Ks, irrespective of their squadron, carried a letter "Q", followed by the "last three" of the USAF serial number. This "Q – code" had previously been applied to the vertical fin of KLU Sabres. In 1961, Sidewinder launch rails were also incorporated onto most aircraft,

known affectionately as the "Kaasjager" ("K"-fighter). The nickname was a play on words as the term also meant "cheese fighter".

Service life of the KLU F-86Ks was relatively short, and a total of thirteen F-86Ks were lost in flying accidents. Starting on 21 June 1962, a number of high-time Sabres were permanently withdrawn from use and sent to Fiat for reconditioning. At the time it was thought that they would be passed on to the Turkish Air Force, but in reality all these aircraft (up to ten) were instead assigned to the Italian AF. The F-86K was officially withdrawn from KLU service on 31 October 1964. Many of the Sabre personnel converted en masse to the Starfighter, but the old F-86K squadron numbers were never reactivated.

700 Sqn

In order to prepare the air force for Sabre operations, 700 Squadron was formed at Soesterburg on 1 August 1955. The unit initially called

upon three Meteor trainers to keep aircrews current. During 1959 KLU Sabre operations were consolidated at Twenthe with the arrival of 700 Sqn from Soesterburg.

Delivered in natural metal finish, 700 Squadron Sabres carried "6A-" codes, each aircraft being then assigned an individual suffix number. 700 Sqn was the last KLU F-86K unit to disband, on 30 June 1964.

701 Sqn

On 1 June 1956, 701 Squadron formed at Twenthe, completing the trio of Dutch Sabre units. The unit's Sabres bore a "Y7-" code, each aircraft being then assigned an individual suffix number. 701 Sqn was inactivated during 1963.

At top, 700 Sqn 55-4900 trails its chute on landing at Twenthe AB. It was one of six Fiat-built F-86Ks delivered to the KLU. (Hans Berfelo) Above, line of 700 Sqn and 701 Sqn F-86Ks. (Hans Berfelo) Below, 701 Sqn F-86Ks carried the "Y-7" code during their early service. 54-1252's pilot is wearing a bowler hat. (JMG Gradidge) Bottom, 702 Sqn F-86K 54-1239 wore the "ZX" code originally and was lost in a crash on 16 March 1961. (JMG Gradidge)

702 Sqn

During August 1955, 328 Squadron at Woensdrecht was disbanded and personnel were transferred to Soesterburg to form 702 Sqn, the KLU's Sabre training unit. 702 Sqn transferred to Twenthe in December 1955 in order to accept the first KLU F-86Ks. 54-1277 and 1278 were accepted on 8 December.

702 Sqn aircraft wore "ZX-" codes, each aircraft being assigned an individual suffix number. With the advent of the F-104 Starfighter the Sabre fleet began to wind down, and 702 Sqn, its training commitment complete, disbanded on 1 April 1962. The surviving aircraft were mostly passed to the remaining squadrons.

NORWAY
ROYAL NORWEGIAN
AIR FORCE

Sixty US-built F-86Ks were supplied to the Royal Norwegian Air Force (RNoAF) begining in September 1955, establishing a true all-weather interceptor force in the country for the first time. One of these aircraft was lost during acceptance trials in America. It was not replaced until early 1960, when the final aircraft of the type was delivered. Once accepted in the United States the aircraft were shipped by sea to Short Brothers and Harland's airfield at Belfast, Northern Ireland, and unpacked for flight testing.

Most of the aircraft were ferried to

Norway by RNoAF pilots, but from September 1955 until October 1956, USAFE personnel were also involved in ferrying these aircraft from Belfast to Gardermoen Air Base, near Oslo. Bill Plunk, a USAF pilot with the 513th FIS remembers these missions:

"In 1955 or early 56, a friend of mine (since deceased) and myself ferried two F-86K models from Ireland to Oslo, Norway - landing on a snow-covered runway. As I recall we spent about 5 days in Copenhagen because of "inclement weather". It was a nice 5 days."

Chuck Metz from the Bentwaters-based 512th FIS adds:

"We flew them from Belfast to Norway, via Holland and Denmark. The aircraft were assembled in Belfast, but those flown by our pilots were brought to Bentwaters for a good inspection prior to the trip. We didn't trust the assembly process, but we did trust our maintenance people. Most trips were not eventful, but I had one that was a real corker, and it took me sever-al weeks to get home. I did not ever get the ship to Norway. I sold it to the Danish Air Force, and as far as I know, it may never have flown again. The whole trip was a comedy of happenings, and it might have ended in my death, but for good luck and caution on my part."

Upon receipt, the first aircraft were inspected and allotted to 337 Skv during September of 1955. The squadron had received a dozen Sabres by the end of the year and delivery was completed during September 1956. The US-built aircraft were supplemented by four Fiat-built examples in June 1957. These replaced a similar number destroyed in a fire at Gardermoen on 10 March 1956. On 27 January 1960 one final F-86K was delivered, a belated replacement for the NAA-built example lost during acceptance in America. This final machine was s/n 54-1231, collected from Brindisi in Italy by a Norwegian pilot. The aircraft had arrived at Brindisi on 8 November 1959 and was overhauled by the Italian company S.A.C.A.

Below, Norway made extensive use of hardened underground shelters, seen here being used by 339 Skv Sabres. Steel doors further compartmented these shelters, giving extra protection from bomb blast. (via Duncan Curtis)

In 1958, the F-86Ks often flew with a device installed under the wing to collect radioactive particles in the air. The samples were sent to the Forsvarets Forskningsinstitutt (Defense Research Institute) for analysis. Inspect and Repair as Necessary (IRAN) overhaul of the F-86Ks also began, based on USAF practice, and took place in L.F.K.

hangar B at Gardermoen.

Like many other European nations, Norway put its Sabres through a number of conversion programs. 12-inch wingtip extensions were embodied in 1959, along with TACAN, ILS and Sidewinder missile capability. At this time Martin-Baker ejection seats also began to be

installed in all RNoAF F-86Ks. The British-built seat was tested in 54-1276 ZK-S of 337 Skv, which was flown to England in 1958 for installation trials.

The last F-86Ks were withdrawn from service on 17 January 1968, the majority being scrapped.

332 Skv

332 Skvadron (Skv) began flying the F-86K in autumn 1962, converting from F-86Fs and concurrently moving from Rygge to Bodø to receive the new type. Most of the squadron's F-86Ks came from 337 Skv, many of the outgoing F-86Fs being passed back to USAF and further service under MAP. The first 332 Skv unit commander with F-86Ks was Major

Jens Petter Andersen

In the Autumn of 1963, 332 and 337 Skv merged and continued operating as 332 Skv. The unit code was "AH", painted on the forward fuselage followed by the individual aircraft letter. 332 Skv only flew the F-86K for two years; in mid-1964 all were transferred to 334 Skv. The unit had only lost one aircraft during this time: 54-1236/AH-H, which crashed on 18 March 1963 at Trehjørningen.

334 Skv

334 Skv at Bodø received its first F-86K on 18 August 1960, and began the conversion from F-86Fs. The unit's personnel had previously undertaken conversion training with 337 and 339 Skv at Gardermoen, making the transition easier. The unit used the "RI" code, commencing from RI-A, which was the first aircraft delivered to 334 Skv. As they were replaced, F-86Fs were largely put through overhaul and sent on to further MAP assignment. The unit's first commanding officer was Major A Klette, but he was replaced on 5 September 1961 by Major E.

Schibbye.

In 1963, 339 Skv disbanded, followed by 332 Skv the following year; both units handed over many of their aircraft to 334 Skv. This influx of Sabres meant that the alphabetical coding of aircraft changed to include numbers. Codes in the range RI-1 to RI-17 were applied to cover extra aircraft. Many of these Sabres were slated for scrapping and were struck off charge in December 1964.

334 Skv formed its own aerobatic team in 1965, commanded by Kapt. Olav Aamot. Five of the squadron's aircraft gained red tails for the purpose and the new team was named

Above, 334 Skv Sabre at a British air show in the early '60s. Tail design was top-to-bottom red, white and blue. Red shield on tail was missing the squadron's insignia. Aircraft was either 54-1251 or 54-1338. (Jack Friell)

"Cola Red". Four aircraft took part in the actual displays, which began at Alta in September 1965. In 1967 Kapt. Aasland took over as team leader, but only a few shows were flown, including one at Harstad.

The squadron converted to the F-5 Freedom Fighter in 1967 and the last Sabres were struck off on 17 January 1968.

337 Skv

The first RNoAF unit to receive F-86Ks, 337 Skv, was activated at Gardermoen AB outside Oslo on 1 September 1955 with Major O. Harby commanding. The squadron received its first aircraft, 54-1251, on 12 September in a ceremony attended by Mr. Strong, the US ambassador to Norway. Initial deliveries were slow however, with only two aircraft on strength until mid-October when a further six were assigned. Norwegian markings and squadron codes had been painted onto the aircraft in Belfast, but Shorts had misread the instruction to apply "ZK" squadron codes; instead the first aircraft arrived in Norway with incorrect "ZX" markings. Incredibly, although a telex was sent to Belfast to rectify the situation, further deliveries saw the aircraft applied with "2X" codes. During the spring of 1956 the unit's aircraft were finally repainted with the correct "ZK" code.

337 Skv suffered a major blow on 10 March 1956 when four aircraft, 54-1242, 54-1254, 54-1258 and 54-1265 were destroyed in a hangar fire at Gardermoen. The squadron received further NAA-built aircraft to account for the loss. The first crash followed soon after; 54-1279 2X-T was lost following engine failure near Gardermoen on 27 June 1956. Lt. Kjell Leistad survived the accident.

337 Skv disbanded on 21 August 1963, transferring most of its aircraft and personnel to 332 Skv at Bodø.

Above, 337 Skv Sabres were initially given "2X" code numbers, later replaced with "ZX". 54-1242 was one of four F-86Ks written-off in a hangar fire at Gardermoen on 10 March 1956. (via Norm Taylor) Below, 54-1247 was a Sidewinder-capable aircraft that was also fitted with a Martin Baker ejector seat. Sharkmouth has blue upper gums and red lower gums with white teeth outlined in red. ZK-F was lost in Hafrsfjord on 30 October 1962. (via Norm Taylor) Bottom, 337 Skv F-86K ZK-I with red and white Sharkmouth outlined in red. Aircraft is seen at a base in Germany. (via Fred Freeman)

339 Skv

339 Skv at Gardermoen AB began converting to the F-86K on 13 July 1956 under the command of Major Ingar Johannesen. The unit used the "SI" squadron code and was fully-equipped by the end of the year.

339 Skv disbanded on 1 September 1963, handing over most of its aircraft to 334 Skv.

Above, F-86K 54-1318 served with 339 Skv for only a year before it was lost in a crash at Gardermoen on 23 March 1957. (via Norm Taylor) Below, 339 Skv 54-1312 wears red-white-blue tail design. Fuselage band was red outlined in yellow. Fuselage lance was red with a black head. (via Fred Freeman)

Below, two 2X-coded machines from 337 Skv and two SI-coded aircraft from 339 Skv in flight over Norway. (via Norm Taylor)

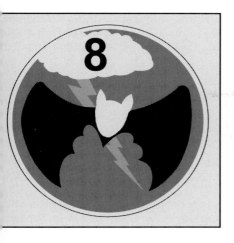

PHILIPPINES
HUKBONG HIMPAPAWID NG PILIPINAS

The Philippine Air Force gained all-weather capability on 12 August 1960 with the delivery of twenty F-86D-36s. Formed at Basa AB as the sole interceptor unit within PAF, 8th Fighter Interceptor Squadron later gained a few more aircraft, including a number of F-86D-50s. Assigned to the 5th Fighter Wing, the F-86Ds were phased out of PAF service in July 1968.

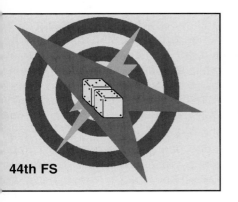

44th FS

TAIWAN

In September 1959, the first of eighteen FEAF F-86D-36s was routed into Shin Meiwa at Komaki, Japan, for overhaul. All of this batch were marked for transfer to Taiwan and the final aircraft was received at Komaki in January 1960. Following overhaul the first two aircraft, 51-6227 and 51-6228, were transferred to the Military Aid Program on 30 August 1960 and subsequently took on ROCAF serials F-86901 and F-86902 respectively. All F-86Ds for the ROCAF were delivered in an overall matt light gray color

Above, Philippine F-86Ds carried no unit markings, just the black-white-red national insignia. (Brian Austria-Tomkins via Bert Anido) Below, two overhauled F-86Ds prior to delivery to Taiwan, Republic of China. The aircraft had a pale gray paint finish applied during overhaul at Komaki, Japan. 51-6245 was landing at NAS Atsugi on 24 October 1960. (T. Matsuzaki) 51-6251 during ferry flight to Taiwan in September 1960. (Pat Murphy via Isham) Bottom, line of ROCAF F-86Ds with 51-6245 in the foreground and fuselage side numbers added. (via Clarence Fu)

scheme, which was retained in service. The last aircraft were delivered on 28 September, and were serialled F-86903 to F-86918 inclusive.

All of the F-86Ds immediately went into service with the 44th Fighter Squadron at Hsinchu AB. Coming under 2nd Fighter Wing control, these

Above, ROCAF F-86Ds had a red intake lip and blue and white rudder stripes and were equipped with Sidewinder launch rails. No side number was applied to 51-8291. (via Burger)

Sabres replaced F-86Fs. Inevitably for such a specialized unit, their service life was short; the remaining F-86Ds were decommissioned in 1966 and the 44th FS became a training unit, inactivating in 1972.

Below, RTAF F-86L 53-718 and sister-ship are seen from a USAF F-102A in 1967. Aircraft were fitted with Sidewinder rocket rails and flew protective top cover for USAF bases in Thailand during the Vietnam War.(USAF)

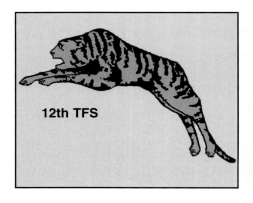

12th TFS

ROYAL THAI AF

Thailand represents a typical example of the misdirection of military aid. Despite having no real need for all-weather interceptor aircraft (Thailand's air force was mainly employed on internal security duties), the Royal Thai Air Force (RTAF) received twenty F-86Ls through MAP in late 1962. No great attempt was made to train Thai pilots and maintenance personnel in the upkeep of the complex aircraft and this later presented problems.

All of the Sabre Dogs supplied to RTAF were ex-US Air National Guard, comprising mainly 124th FIS Iowa ANG aircraft. These airframes were briefly stored at Davis-Monthan AFB from March to April 1962, and they had only recently been retired when the Thai requirement was approved. Many were overhauled at Inglewood prior to assignment to MAP in November 1962. The official delivery of the first 17 was on 28 December 1962. A further aircraft, 53-978, was assigned on 6 November 1963 bringing the initial total to 18 F-86Ls, all dash-55 and

dash–60 models.

The delivery of the F-86Ls allowed 12 Squadron to equip with the type. The unit's F-86Fs at Don Muang were assigned to a new unit, 43 Squadron at Takhli AB. In Thai service, the F-86Ls were referred to as "Boh Koh 17g", and dedicated Thai serials were assigned, ranging from Kh17g-1/06 to Kh17g-18/06 for the first batch. In addition to the RTAF serials, 12 Sqn applied its own code numbers to the aircraft, apparently denoting flight assignment. The codes were 1211-1215, 1221-1224, 1231-1234 and 1241-1244, inclusive.

Two further F-86Ls were delivered on 28 January 1966, and these aircraft, 53-557 and 53-920, were given the Thai serial numbers Kh17g-19/09 and Kh17g-20/09, respectively. They too joined 12 Squadron where they took on the codes 1235 and 1245.

Thailand was the only nation outside the United States to operate the F-86L. However, Thailand was not supplied with the "SAGE" equipment to support their intended role, and

spares backup in general was poor. The 12 Squadron F-86Ls proved a maintenance nightmare for the Thais, and within a year of their arrival an American report stated that only two aircraft remained in commission, while a further three had not even been assembled. Further to this, in 1967 a US Army Audit Agency report declared that, "as of 30 June 1966, the [F-86L] squadron has never been rated operationally ready for combat since receipt of the aircraft in December 1962." Nonetheless, the RTAF continued to declare the squadron as operational, though a 1969 US General Accounting Office report stated that these jets had not "contributed greatly to the realization of primary US objectives."

At least one aircraft was written off in Thai service; 53-978 crashed into the Chao Phraya River near Pak Kret in July 1965 and was not recovered. The F-86Ls were officially retired from Thai service on 28 June 1967. Wisely, the Thai Air Force learnt from its earlier mistakes and procured (along with MAP-supplied F-5s) propeller-driven aircraft for internal security policing.

Above, all RTAF F-86Ls wore the same smart 12 squadron scheme. The tail band was medium blue with white shooting stars, bordered by white and black stripes. The wing tips were also blue and the squadron's "leaping tiger" was painted on the forward fuselage. (via Duncan Curtis) At right, RTAF F-86Ls were retired in June 1967, and the aircraft remained parked at Don Muang for some time. They were still there on 16 November 1967. (Friell)

VENEZUELA

During 1965, the Fuerza Aerea Venezolana (FAV) began negotiations with the West German government for the purchase of all surviving Luftwaffe F-86Ks, including the unflown examples, which amounted to 73 examples. Export licences were approved for 51 aircraft (presumably the airworthy ones), and the sale was worth £50,000 ($140,000) per aircraft, including spares. It was reported at the time that the deal included the fitting of reconnaissance equipment in some aircraft, but no evidence can be found to substantiate this. Seventy-eight F-86Ks were eventually supplied to the FAV, including many unused, non-flyable aircraft as spares sources. At least four aircraft being shipped by sea were impounded at the docks in Curaçao on delivery and never made it into service. They were eventually moved to Albert Plesman Airport for use by the fire department and subsequently scrapped while still in their

USAF delivery markings. These aircraft were 55-4866, 55-4901, 55-4910 and 55-4913.

On 27 July 1961, the FAV had reorganized and created Grupo Aereo de Caza (GAC - Air Fighter Group) No. 12 at El Liberatador Air Base near Palo Negro in the northern part of the country. It was formed with three existing Fighter units: Escadron de Caza 34 "Caciques", equipped with Venom aircraft, Esc de Caza 35

"Panteras" equipped with Vampires and Esc de Caza 36 "Jaguares" equipped with F-86F Sabres. The first Commander of GAC No. 12 was Lieutenant Colonel Alberto Vivas Serrano.

At the end of 1966, the F-86Ks began arriving at GAC No.12, giving it a new mission – that of interception. The F-86Ks replaced the Vampires of Esc de Caza 35, but almost immediately hit problems; the complexity of

the aircraft made it less than ideal for use when minimal technical support was available. The F-86Ks encountered many maintenance problems, and a large number were grounded in July 1969 because of hydraulic hose faults. At best only thirty or more aircraft were ever declared as fit for use.

All Venezuelan F-86Ks were finished in a pale gray overall paint scheme, with just the "roundel and bar" insignia and tail stripes identifying the aircraft. The FAV serial system, comprising a seemingly random set of four numbers, was applied to the fin of each aircraft. These numbers ranged from 0002 (55-4895) to 5627 (56-4158). They appear to have been allotted in USAF serial number order.

In July 1971, GAC No. 12 moved to Tte. Vicente Landaeta Gil AB, Barquisimeto, reorganizing with just two squadrons: Esc 36 with F-86Fs, and the F-86Ks of Esc 35. Esc 34 was deactivated. At the end of 1971, negotiations for the acquisition of CF-5 aircraft began and these arrived at the beginning of 1972, allowing the replacement of the F-86Ks in Esc 35.

Four FAV F-86Ks were transferred to the Honduran AF following overhaul. It seems likely that this event occurred some time after 1975. Surviving FAV aircraft were withdrawn at Palo Negro and most are still there, slowly rotting away.

At top, freshly painted 0943 in standard FAV colors were light gray with national insignia across the tail. Top to bottom; yellow, dark blue, red. (Mick Roth) Above left, flight of six FAV F-86Ks marked as 0843 at top. Although washed out by the sun's reflection, all the aircraft wear FAV in capital letters mid-way across the upper right wing. (John Lake) Above Left, Louis Santos and friends refurbishing one of two F-86Ks for static display. The pale gray base color has been applied to the fuselage. (Louis Santos) At left, when put on static display, many FAV Sabres received camouflage schemes, in this case three colors of gray with a red and white sharkmouth. (via Duncan Curtis)

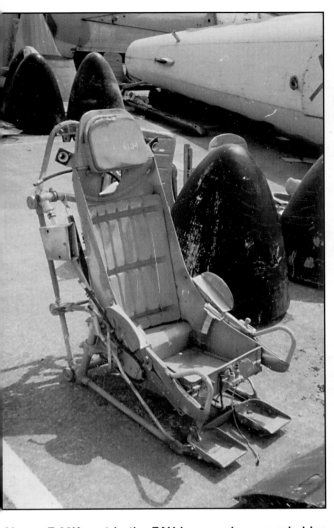

Above, F-86K seat in the FAV boneyard surrounded by radomes. At right top, two of the FAV "K"s minus radomes await their fate. Above right, another F-86K awaits preservation or scrapping. Above right, the bone yard treasure trove; many of the F-86K wings in the foreground were spares and had never been used. At right, one of the F-86Ks that was restored to static display in original gray color by Louis Santos and friends. Below, another restored "K", this time in a gray and brown scheme. (all photos Louis Santos)

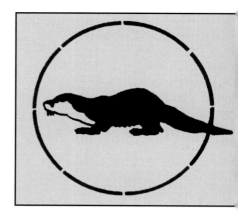

YUGOSLAVIA

Yugoslavia's Ratnog Vazduhoplovstva i ProtivVazdusne Odbrane (RV i PVO - Air Force and Anti Aircraft Defense) had operated Canadair Sabre 4s since 1956 and in the early 1960s also began to receive F-86D aircraft. However, due to Yugoslavia's warming relations with the Eastern Bloc, these aircraft were not supplied gratis. Instead they had to be purchased outright. This proved a double-edged sword for the west, as it meant that the RV i PVO could use the aircraft for whatever purpose it wished.

The newly-acquired F-86Ds were delivered straight from the 3130th Air Base Group at Chateauroux Air Base in France starting in late July 1961, and initially passed to depot organization "Jastreb" for repair and maintenance. 130 F-86Ds were delivered, comprising 15 F-86D-36s, 25 F-86D-

41s, 53 F-86D-45s and 37 F-86D-50s; they were assigned consecutive RV i PVO serials from 14001 (USAF 51-6147) to 14130 (52-10130). Final aircraft were assigned to MAP for the Yugoslavs on 20 November 1961.

Straight away, thirty Sabres were diverted for spares use, though it seems that most of this batch – the final few delivered – were later slated for conversion into reconnaissance versions.

The Yugoslavs soon discovered that none of the aircraft had E-4 radar fitted, which was essential to the aircraft's operation. Also, there were no supplies of Mighty Mouse rockets, the F-86D's only armament. Following protests from Yugoslavia, the US Government arranged for the delivery of this missing equipment.

The first unit of the RV i PVO to receive the F-86D was 117 vazduh-

plovni puk (vp - fighter wing) at Batajnica, which had been flying the F-86E. Wing personnel completed their F-86D ground training at the "Jastreb" repair depot during August 1962. Flight training began on 5 September the same year, and by the end of 1962, this training had in turn been successfully completed, by this time the eskadrilles (squadrons) of 117 vp had ten F-86Ds in service. Further F-86Ds were delivered to the Wing in 1963, when 117 vp displayed the aircraft to the public for the first time at the May Day Parade in Belgrade. By the end of 1963, 117 vp had thirty-one F-86Ds at its disposal.

Because of the complexity of the F-86D's electrical systems, and its relatively advanced engine systems, the RV i PVO aircraft technicians were not entirely enamoured with the aircraft. Frequent unserviceabilities required an inordinate amount of man-hours to maintain the F-86D, and cannibalization was the order of the day. Even though the Yugoslavs had purchased more than one hundred F-86Ds, the number in operational service rarely exceeded forty. RV i PVO F-86Ds were generally left unpainted, with anti-dazzle panels either olive drab or black. A camouflage scheme was also adopted, and F-86Ds in this scheme were often seen without the anti-dazzle panel.

At left, many Yugoslav F-86Ds were camouflaged in a green and gray scheme. Tail stripes were, top-to-bottom, blue, white and red with a red star painted on the white stripe. 14029 was F-86D-41 52-3717. (via Duncan Curtis)